HEAR Her NOW

POSITIVE PERSPECTIVES ON WOMEN COMING INTO THEIR POWER

COMPILED BY
Cathy L. Davis

Hear Her Now
Positive Perspectives on Women Coming Into Their Power
UpsiDaisy Press

Published by **UpsiDaisy Press**, St. Louis, MO
Copyright ©2018 Cathy L. Davis
All rights reserved.

No part of this publication may be reproduced, stored in a retrieval system, or transmitted in any form or by any means, electronic, mechanical, photocopying, recording, scanning, or otherwise, except as permitted under Section 107 or 108 of the 1976 United States Copyright Act, without the prior written permission of the Publisher. Requests to the Publisher for permission should be addressed to Cathy@daviscreative.com, please put **Hear Her Now** in the subject line.

Limit of Liability/Disclaimer of Warranty: While the publisher and authors have used their best efforts in preparing this book, they make no representations or warranties with respect to the accuracy or completeness of the contents of this book and specifically disclaim any implied warranties of appropriateness or merchantability for a particular purpose. The advice and strategies contained herein may not be suitable for your situation. You should consult with a professional where appropriate. Neither the publisher nor author shall be liable for any loss of profit or any other commercial damages, including but not limited to special, incidental, consequential, or other damages.

All contributing authors to this anthology have submitted their chapters to an editing process, and have accepted the recommendations of the editors at their own discretion. All authors have approved their chapters prior to publication.

Cover and Interior design: Davis Creative, DavisCreative.com

Hear Her Now
ISBN: 978-0-9774886-6-7

Table of Contents

FOREWORD/Cathy Davis
Finding Her Power...1

Celeste Hartwell
Healing Through Writing..7

Kara Hanak
Finding My Tribes..13

Shannon Shores
Conductor of the Hot Mess Express........................21

Kristy Barton
Hope..27

Mary Kausch
Becoming A Force of Nature...................................35

Debi Corrie
Waiting for Success..41

Pam Wilson
Freedom...49

Lisa Bobyak
*The Three Lies that Kept me from Living the
Life I was Designed for*..55

Sandy Tomey
The Power of the Sacred Love Journey....................63

Gina Nicole Ballard
Guiding Angels and Embracing Your Intuition.........71

Dr. Heidi Brocke
Feel the Freedom 79

Dena B. Tranen
Minding Your Way... 85

Anna-Marie Beard
And That's Okay.. 91

Cynthia Steinert
The Leap 99

Rebecca Now
American Women Speak Up 105

FOREWORD

CATHY DAVIS

Finding Her Power

It wasn't until I had my own business that I stopped to reflect on the entrepreneurial influence of my childhood. Generations of women before me stepped into their power by not only finding ways to contribute to the family income, but quite often became the primary breadwinner when husbands/fathers/sons/brothers went off to war—AND even continued in that role when they came back.

My great-grandparents had a coffee-shop/restaurant in their home town of Dexter, Kansas. Stories tell of how my great-grandmother, Nancy Miller, started it by serving meals to her out-of-work neighbors out of the kitchen at the back of her home during the Great Depression. Word got out she was a pretty good cook. Soon people started showing up who could pay her, and eventually they moved to a downtown storefront.

Nancy was also the mother of 13 children (11 surviving childbirth) in a 4-room house. THE SAME house where she was feeding neighbors and strangers out her back door. THE SAME house which did not have an indoor toilet until the early 1900's!

My grandmother, Margaret (nicknamed Peggy), was the second-eldest of those 13 children. Peggy and her husband, John, also had a restaurant for a short while. Many of Peggy's 11 siblings were barbers, beauticians, ranchers, farmers, mechanics, bakers, florists—all finding a way to survive the Great Depression. As a small child, I was surrounded by adults working for themselves. The message I received was simple: "If you can't find a job, find a way to make money."

Peggy saw World War I as a teenager, and the Great Depression as a young wife. Her daughter, Jean (my Mother), saw World War II as a teenager and young wife. The men went off to war, and the women were left in charge of not only the home and the kids, but of adding to the family income. The role of women in the household and the workplace was changing.

The messages I received as a child—of women coming into their own power—were reflected not only through my family ties, but also through the sitcoms I saw on television. As I grew up, I watched a progression of TV shows showing women coming into their own power throughout the decades. In the 1950's, we watched "Father Knows Best," where everyone did what Dad told them to do. In the 1960's we were introduced to "The Dick Van Dyke Show," where Mary asked Dick if she could work part-time. In the 1970's we saw the spin-off, "The Mary Tyler Moore Show", where Mary found her own career, had her own apartment and lived alone—quite happily. The 1980's brought us Murphy Brown, where having a baby out of wedlock while holding down a full-time, high-profile job became the topic of discussion around the neighborhood as well as in politics. "The Golden Girls," "Friends," "Sex and the City," and "Will and Grace" brought us into the 21st century with even more roles being well-defined, if not reversed.

In grade school, my neighborhood friends and I would play "office" and "grocery store," and sometimes even "architect" and "restaurant." Somehow, I always knew I would be working for myself. I just wasn't sure how to make that happen.

Looking back, most of my corporate career was spent involved with marketing high-net-worth financial services. It wasn't planned, I just ended up there. Although the financial services industry has changed over the years, back in the 1990s, it was still very much a male-dominant institution. Luckily, I got to experience both male and female managers, and at one point, I too became a manager of a staff of 18. I not only got to experience the changing roles of women in the workplace, I truly feel I was able to contribute to making a positive impact on the roles of women in corporate culture. I have kept in contact with several of my former staff and a few years ago, I received a very nice note from one, which I cherish to this day…

"I just want to thank you for being my manager… our many conversations have stayed with me all these years later, and how you managed ME with such compassion continues to influence how I manage others to this day. From managing staff and vendors, to the one-on-one conversations with my children—somehow, I'm able to reflect upon your patience and professionalism and use what I learned from you in my relationships today. Thank you!"

Having a team, creating common goals, and celebrating the accomplishment of those goals is what I miss the most about corporate life. Yet, after experiencing two downsizings in less than 5 years, I was determined to find my own path and never walk back into the corporate culture again. Somewhere within my DNA was a determination to start and grow a business that would support me and my family in a comfortable lifestyle. I was ready to "find a way to make money" as did the generations before me.

It was December of 2003 when I walked away from the comfort of a corporate paycheck. And, although I'd love to be able to say it's all been a piece-of-cake, what I CAN say as we approach our 15th anniversary, is that the one thing I've learned the most is…

When I trust myself and my intuition,
it allows me to grow in confidence and step into my own power.
Stepping into my own power allows me to use my voice,
share my talents, and create positive
ripples in the lives of the people I reach.

The following chapters have all been written by women who have followed their own path—even when that path may have been unexpected—with dips and turns, or mountains and valleys. Each has found their own way through trials and tribulations, and are a tribute to women everywhere who may be in the middle of a struggle, or who have found their way through the latest darkness—stronger for the journey, and wiser for the experience.

May you find yourself and your strength, within the power of these stories.

Finding Her Power

Cathy Davis is the CEO of Davis Creative, a branding services agency headquartered in St Louis, MO, specializing in brand strategy, graphic design and independent publishing. With clients in all 50 states, Davis Creative is known for helping purpose-driven clients Look Good, Attract More Clients and Monetize Their Passion.

As a professional branding and author consultant, books and publishing have always been an integral part of Cathy's life—from making them as a student in college, to working for a major book retailer after college, to collecting them for her personal library. A former board member of the St. Louis Publisher's Association, she began introducing her clients to the power of self-publishing in 2005.

Cathy L. Davis
cathy@DavisCreative.com
www.DavisCreative.com
www.facebook.com/DavisCreativeLLC/
www.linkedin.com/in/cathyldavis/

CELESTE HARTWELL

Healing Through Writing

When I was young, I found comfort in writing.
I grew up in what I knew as a normal household; there was yelling, screaming, abuse and emotional manipulation. There were unhappy people everywhere I turned.

Some family members hid it better than others. Based on this observation, one of the first pieces I wrote when I was twelve years old spoke about pictures of a family, with everyone looking happy and how that was not the truth.

Thus, my basis of how life was supposed to be: "look" happy but don't let anyone dig too deep under the surface.

However, this did not bode well for my Scorpio nature. A natural seeker, I grew up continually seeking and searching for something better, something more, and I continued to find solace in the words.

The writing allowed me to reach deeper parts of myself I wasn't able to access through talking or thinking. The words helped me process through the murkiness of ongoing depression, self-hatred, and pain. Reading what I had written helped me see what I was struggling with in a way I hadn't been able to previously.

As I grew older, I was getting the cosmic nudge to share my words with people on a larger scale despite my fear. I had seen the power of sharing my experiences before, so I followed the guidance and shared again.

I was on stage at an event, sharing a profoundly vulnerable piece I had written.

My legs and voice were shaking. I gripped the paper tightly as I spoke into the microphone and barely took my eyes off the page under the harsh lights against the black night.

"We met in non-physical, you and I. Among the cosmic stars and dust, our energy fields, our souls were friends."

I go on to describe the soul agreement I believe my mother and I made before our coming into this lifetime and which forged this mother/daughter relationship.

The piece goes on to talk about how much hell she would put me through, how she would consider aborting me before my birth, how that would wreak havoc on my self-esteem and worthiness for years to come.

I bring up memories of how she punched and kicked me, attempted to drag me down the stairs by my feet, held razor blades up to me and dared me to kill her when I was a teenager.

Throughout the entire poem, she lovingly continually repeats "I will do anything for you."

I then go on to tell my mother of the trauma she will need to go through to put me through the abuse she does - how my mother will withstand sexual abuse from a sickeningly young age, how she will be beaten and bruised, violated physically, emotionally, spiritually and sexually.

I relay that she will have to go through hell and back, repeated sexual trauma and a nightmare of a life, for her to treat me the way she does so I can learn these lessons.

She agrees to do that for me.

Then I tell her about how we come back around, how she is my greatest teacher in helping me learn compassion, forgiveness, and empathy. My poem ends with a very heartfelt appreciation and love for her role in my life.

In the black of night, there are wails in the audience, women reliving their own abuses and hell, crying out in the night and finding healing in the loving embrace of the spiritual and profoundly connected audience.

Later that evening, and in the days following, I learned how much power our words have. Women approached me long after the event to tell me how pivotal that share was in their healing process and their lives.

By hearing someone outside of themselves, who was able to verbalize their turmoil in such a concise way, it allowed them to process through their own emotions and experiences.

My realization after I shared this piece of my soul: despite my deep-rooted fears around sharing, being visible and knowing it would be triggering for so many women in the audience, this piece was healing for the women who were going to hear it. It was my responsibility to allow them to have that experience so they could see the pain to heal it.

What I have learned is that our writing not only heals our wounds, but when we share our experiences, they can heal the world. What my sharing of this particular piece, on that stage, cemented was the knowledge I already had: By using my words, my voice, my gifts, I was helping other women to step into their gifts, use their voice and heal not only themselves but others as well.

Here is what I know for sure: we as women must find our voice and communicate our wants and needs in a way that is loving, compassionate and kind because if we don't speak from our heart, no one will hear us.

We must voice our needs lovingly and respectfully so that we create allies and help others to understand what they need to do to help make this world a better place.

Once we can connect into our own words and our unique voice, we will be able to spread more love far and wide and help end the fear mentality that is so rampant in our culture. I believe for a fact that by sharing our experiences and voicing our words through love, we will be able to end sex trafficking, school shootings, and sexual assault.

I believe that for a long time, women have been silent about the injustices that have been happening to them. Sometimes it has been because we haven't known how to voice it or didn't know if anyone would hear it.

That time is over. People are standing up, listening, learning and taking action to make this world a better place.

Therefore, it is essential now more than ever, to share our voice through writing and a big reason why I am so passionate about helping women find their voice through their writing. Whether it is through getting to know their unique writing style, or through writing a book in four-and-a-half days, it is time for us to communicate in healthy ways, that will move the planet and consciousness forward.

Healing Through Writing

As a Certified Holistic Health Coach, relationship guru and book coach, **Celeste Hartwell** is both humbled and deeply appreciative to be a part of the "Hear Her Now" Anthology.

Celeste believes in the power of women in community, and focuses on empowering women through her individual and group coaching programs, workshops, retreats and classes she teaches.

With a passion for helping women and young ladies find their voices so they can live their best lives, Celeste is in the process of creating a magazine to empower young ladies to know they are capable of doing anything they want to do.

She loves working with women of all ages and walks of life to help them find their inner wisdom through their words and to empower them to become the leaders they are capable of becoming.

Celeste Hartwell
celeste@divinefeminineleaders.com
www.divinefeminineleaders.com
www.whatgirlsdo.com
www.facebook.com/hartwellceleste
www.instagram.com/hartwellceleste

KARA HANAK

Finding My Tribes

Have you ever looked around and wondered how you were lucky enough to be surrounded by great people? The last time this occurred to me, I was posing with a giant inflatable unicorn surrounded by women from every important time in my life. No, this wasn't a psychedelic, drug-induced dream; rather, it was a unicorn-themed fortieth birthday party that provided one of the clearest revelations of how truly fortunate I am.

In the spirit of true unicorn magic, the stars and calendars aligned, and now the most important people from all the phases of my life collided in one place; no longer would I be able to get away with keeping the familiar characters separated through my many stories. The days leading up to the party were almost as terrifying as exciting—the Tribes were officially meeting.

I call them Tribes because these are the people you call when your toddler sticks a bean up her nose—they know how to remove it and will laugh when it's over (without judgment). These are the women you text first when you get a promotion and are full of new job euphoria. They are the ones you cry with when you face the death of one of your own. We've celebrated triumphs, agonized over loss, and laughed until our faces and abs couldn't take any more. These women have been by my side through the pits of despair to my most joyful moments. They have often gently guided me, more than once carried me, and occasionally flat-out dared me to be the best leader I can be. They inspire me. Every. Day.

These Tribes are my people, and this birthday was a celebration of the joy, compassion, and wisdom that they built in me. Though most had never physically met, the Tribes have been instrumental in forming the five core tenants of leadership that guide me through almost all aspects of life. I call them the five ships: fellowship, relationship, mentorship, scholarship, and stewardship.

As I looked around the room, I spotted my friend JT on the back porch. While we met in high school, we often joke that we have now been friends longer than we didn't know each other. Today we share work, weddings, and wineries, but back then I was a nerdy, socially-awkward, introvert trying to fit into a world of extroverted high school students. As I nostalgically reflect on that time of my life, even though I participated in school athletics and clubs, I struggled to figure out where I fit. One mid-August afternoon, I found myself dripping wet from a brief rain shower in Mile High Stadium with more than 50,000 other high school students watching a helicopter land under one of the most brilliant rainbows I had ever seen. The event was not a ballgame or a concert, it was the kickoff for the 1993 World Youth Day. Over the course of that week, I met youth from around the country and around the world. At that time, I didn't have a word for the sense of belonging I felt, but I recognize it now as *fellowship*. When I returned home from that experience, I took a more active role in leading in the Belleville Diocesan Catholic Youth Organization (CYO). CYO was my first tribe.

Expanding on my new sense of fellowship, I campaigned for and was elected to be the organization's regional and national representative. CYO offered my first official large leadership opportunity and gave me a taste of how gratifying leadership could be. I spent the majority of my remaining high school free time traveling the 12,000 square miles of southern Illinois and organizing people and events to share that camaraderie. As an adult,

Finding My Tribes

I have found that fellowship with a group of people with similar interests, goals, or purpose remains important. It fosters trust, expands loyalty, assumes the best of intentions, and forgives minor missteps that enable growth—all critical components in each of the next tribes in my life.

Gathered around the kitchen table sat a group of besties that I had known for over two decades. Christy, Amy, Christine, Jen, and Annie are my Dominican Tribe. We were introduced at college orientation—some of us as new freshmen, others established campus leaders—and little did we know that those introductions would cement lifelong *relationships*. These ladies have been with me through most of my best times and several of my most difficult.

At seventeen, I left home for college and struggled to make the adjustment from growing up in rural America to big city living. After a tear-filled first semester and serious thoughts about transferring closer to home, I instead came back after winter break resolved to make it work; I threw myself into leadership positions in residential life and student government. I anchored myself by growing closer with the fun, loyal women I had met at orientation. Our friendships matured through enduring early classes, a love of Tracy Chapman music, innocuous pranks, and the occasional breaking of a few minor rules. My Dominican Tribe introduced me to diversity, drove me to cement career decisions, and helped me learn how to navigate difficult situations. Unfortunately, we also learned just a little bit later in life how to endure heartbreak when one of our own unexpectedly gained her angel wings, leaving a hole in our collective hearts. Early on, we took for granted having Mary (Sunshine) as the glue that held us all together. In the years since her passing, her memory serves as an important reminder that it is our job to maintain our precious relationships with love, compassion, and a commitment to show up for the important things, especially unicorn fortieth birthday parties.

In the kitchen, my friend Katy was busy ensuring her birthday party project plan was executed to perfection. Katy is part of a tribe I lovingly dubbed the Super Ninjas Tribe. The Super Ninjas formed in late 2014, on a day that was anything but super. A set of layoffs large enough to make local news had restructured a substantial portion of our department, and with it reshaped my strategic program management team. Katy, Krista, Ashley, Jackie, and I went out to lunch at one of our favorite Indian buffets that day, and little did we know that this lunch was actually the start of something spectacular. Over the course of the next few lightning quick years, these women solved large corporate problems, positively impacted millions of patients' lives, and made it all look effortless. A week never went by without my inbox receiving a note of praise for one of the Super Ninjas.

My time with the Super Ninjas taught me the benefits of *mentorship*. In this team of top performers, each with Achiever as one of the top five in their StrengthsFinder profile, there was easily the potential for me to spend my weeks breaking up sparring matches between teammates competing to be at the top. But that just wasn't these women. Instead, I spent my time figuring out how to maximize our strengths and emphasizing strong internal team support and cross-pollination. Consequently, the team flourished, each growing skills in areas that led to great next career steps. As our time together neared an end, I began to feel a huge sense of pride that all of the time we had spent in our one-on-one meetings soul-searching, planning, and navigating had led each of these women to the verge of finding her next dream role. I relished in getting to send out brag notes for five promotions, a move to one of the "Best Places to Work" in St. Louis, and a return to a team that desperately needed guidance and organization that could not be delivered by anyone else. While I was the "official" leader of this team, I learned that building a top performing team requires that everyone on the team wants to learn from each other and see the team succeed as a whole.

I turned to the living room and saw that it had been overrun by children—seventeen of them, all under twelve—playing with the giant inflatable unicorn. These kids are our future, and none of them came with an instruction manual, my two included. This is where I reach out to my Mama Bear Tribe. These are the women that gather to walk the track during soccer practice, bring an extra coffee to the early morning basketball game, and graciously ignore my imperfect house to show up in their favorite comfy clothes for girls night in. On this day, Amber, my favorite life cheerleader, was representing Maria, Kim, Andrea, Annette, Jen, and Wendy from team Mama Bear. These ladies have taught me when to not worry about getting bit at daycare, when I should worry about pre-teen girls, and just about everything in between. While our friendships were naturally born as a result of our children, we have been through family, kids, career, and life changes together. As a woman who has spent more than her fair share of time in a formal classroom and thrives on being a lifelong learner, this Tribe has expanded my view on *scholarship*. I no longer view it as just traditional learning but how to use a growth mindset to learn about life together and from each other.

As a result of learning with and from each of these Tribes, I am driven to build loyalty via fellowship, nurture relationships, practice mentorship, and foster my love of learning through scholarship. Ironically, in the spirit of the founder of the former Boy Scouts of America, Lord Robert Baden-Powell, these *women* have helped me embrace the philosophy of *stewardship*—leaving the world a little better than you found it. In big and in small ways, they push me to be a better leader every day—to leave each person or team I interact with better positioned for their personal success and how they want (and will continue) to change the world. As I look at the future, I know and trust that the strong, dedicated, powerful women of my current and future Tribes will continue to be wildly successful.

To the ladies of my Tribes: that inflatable unicorn is stored away for safekeeping, and I look forward to frequently breaking it out to celebrate your successes.

Kara Green Hanak is a talent maximizer, innovation enthusiast, and not-so-closet techie. Throughout her career, she's applied broad learnings from her experience in technology, program management, strategy, and analytics to fuel her true passion—leadership.

Kara has led teams in the consulting, technology, financial services, and healthcare industries. Some of her most memorable career moments include growing from manager to senior director throughout her 10 years at Express Scripts, leading a 120-person team through a post-merger integration impacting over half of the company's customers, and guiding the Super Ninjas to successfully launch 100 innovation initiatives in three years.

In an effort to continually expand her tribes, Kara has sought out multiple leadership opportunities in the community, including being selected into the FOCUS Leadership St. Louis program, an immersive experience that explores community opportunities and challenges. However, Kara takes the most pride in the coaching she provides to women seeking mentorship on the path to growing in their own careers. Kara has a genuine ability to meet other women where they are, connect through personal stories, and bring out the confidence and skills needed to maximize their potential. In the coming years, Kara looks forward to expanding her passion for leadership and coaching into new opportunities.

Kara lives in St. Louis, Missouri, with her Ohana Tribe, Will (12) and Savannah (10). She enjoys photography, wine and ethnic foods, conquering her ever-expanding bucket list, and being surrounded by her Tribes.

Kara Green Hanak
www.linkedin.com/in/kara-hanak

SHANNON SHORES

Conductor of the Hot Mess Express

Yes! I am the conductor of the Hot Mess Express. I am in charge of getting this train called life down the tracks. At times, I have wanted to stop the train. There were plenty of times I wanted to pull out the puke bag because I have gotten motion sick from all the unexpected movement along the track.

Just like many of you, I rush out of the house every day. I pull into the drop-off lane at my kids' school on two wheels as I am always running late. I am sure my time-management would be better with the lack of missing shoes, fights over who gets to use the bathroom first, or what to eat for breakfast. I am convinced that the school traffic lady curses me under her breath while I am rolling my kids out of the car, cleaning their faces from the breakfast they ate in the car with my shirt or a spit bath. I swore I would never give my kids a spit bath, but I guess I never imagined how messy boys would be! I try my best with my children. I wonder if they were to grade me what they would say.

So, I share this story as many say it is full of encouragement and grace. For me it is a story of finding strength and love and reclaiming my faith.

I grew up in church. I attended every Sunday and heard the stories on how God worked miracles. I knew of God, but I didn't personally know him until many years later. In fact, for many years I was mad at God. I felt lost and abandoned by him.

There was a time when my mind was consumed with self-doubt, fear, and confusion. All my life I just wanted to be "normal" and "happy." I really didn't know what that meant, but I hoped I would know it when I found it.

Fourteen years ago, I was pregnant with my first child. I remember how excited yet scared I was to become a mother. I often questioned if I was prepared enough. Would I know what to do? Was I unselfish enough to take on the biggest job of my life?

I remember getting the first ultrasound of my tiny peanut of love and those doubts fading away. I fell in love immediately. I knew at that point I would do everything in my power to be the best momma in the world. I spent the next several weeks falling more in love.

At my second trimester appointment check-up I was so excited to see my love and hear the progress. The ultrasound tech came in and my excitement felt like it was going to burst. My baby's pictures appeared on the screen. The mood in the room immediately changed. The once chatty tech had become silent. All I could hear was the sound of her mouse as she stared deeply into her monitor. She finally turned to me and said, "The doctor will be in soon." I knew this was bad. I was in shock and horrified about what would happen next.

The doctor entered the room, tapped me on the leg and said, "I am so sorry. Your baby has died. Your body hasn't recognized it yet so go home and let nature do its thing."

I walked out of the hospital numb. I replayed his words in my head to make sure that I heard him correctly. It was the longest four days of my life. Nature didn't do its thing and I ended up having a D&C, still hopeful that they would discover that the doctor was wrong. Sadly, he was right.

The following months were brutal. I was a functional depressed person. I would get up in the morning, put on a smile for the world and come home and crash. For months, I would work, cry, sleep, and repeat. At times, suicidal thoughts passed through my mind. My heart hurt so bad that I just wanted to go to sleep and never wake up.

Many people reached out to me with thoughts of, "It wasn't in God's plan," or "Let go, let God." These words infuriated me.

"Yea, God, where are you? This sadness is your plan? How could you do this to me? You have blessed others with babies, but you take mine away!" I cried out when alone.

The reason why the words others used to console me hurt was because my faith was missing. I made inaccurate assumptions about God. It wasn't until years later that I would appreciate those phrases and personally use them to get through dark times. With the help of a therapist and psychiatric care, I made it, but there isn't a September 27 that I don't think about my sweet angel.

I sit looking through my emotional suitcase. Each moment is tucked away neatly and carefully. I still see my psychiatrist a couple times each year. She often questions this emotional suitcase that I carry. She acknowledges great changes but has concerns about what would happen if that suitcase ever tips over. Will I be ready?

Those moments in the suitcase haunted me for years. It was like when I was a kid. When I went to my room at night, I would turn off my light and run as fast as I could to jump into bed because I was afraid of the monsters under my bed. As I got older, I found myself still afraid of those monsters.

At this point, God had blessed me with two beautiful and healthy boys. I was figuring out the mom thing, but my marriage was crumbling. I felt like a failure. I wondered why I wasn't enough. What could I do differently or better? I found myself turning into a detective searching for the answers. I found the answer in a sign hanging in a church my friend invited me to attend. It read, "God didn't promise you days without pain, laughter without sorrow, or sun without rain, but he did promise strength for the day, comfort for the tears, and light for the way." I remember reading that sign and thinking to myself, "God must think that I am Wonder Woman."

The following day I woke up and that sign kept appearing in my head. I thought "Maybe God is here." Is it possible that our current situation is tough, but God is shielding me and my boys from pain and danger? Is this part of the plan? I was carrying my laundry basket up the stairs and my newborn baby was crying. I felt overwhelmed and not strong enough for the road that was ahead of me. I threw that laundry basket at the bathroom door. My nicely, folded laundry went everywhere, and I dropped to my knees crying to the Lord. "Here I am, Lord. Please help me!" I know people talk about hearing God's voice, but for me I felt an immediate sense of relief as I felt God saying, "I have been waiting, so glad you called me."

God helped me through that storm. During the time of a painful divorce and loss of my sons' father, I found myself. When my life was falling apart, it was actually falling together. I learned that I could not hold myself accountable for anyone else's actions any longer. Nor could I love someone out of something.

After this, I thought I would never love again. I put up an electric fence around my heart. With the encouragement of a friend, I made a list of characteristics I wanted in a partner. Then, when I met someone, I could compare him to my list. I wanted to make that description impossible—like a man with one purple eye and the other green. My heart would not allow it. I prayed to God for a partner. I wanted to be a penguin. I wanted to find my mate for life. I wanted someone to help me raise my most precious gifts, my sons.

God had faith in me yet again. He sent a selfless man who wouldn't give up. He was determined to get past the electric fence of my heart and he helped me unpack my emotional suitcase. This man would wipe my tears, never give up on me, and is an amazing father to our boys.

True love stories have no endings.

People often ask how I navigated unpacking my emotional suitcase. I take it one moment at a time. I won't allow anyone to break me. I remember to love myself and surround myself with people who fill my suitcase with love. This is me: the woman I am now, no longer afraid of the monsters under the bed and the conductor of the Hot Mess Express.

Hear Her Now

Shannon Shores earned her master's in social work from Southern Illinois University Carbondale. She has utilized her social work skills to operate Wellex Inc. which powers samedaystdtesting.com. As CEO of Wellex Inc., she runs a nationwide call center to help people receive confidential and reliable testing for sexually transmitted diseases. Wellex Inc started in 2015 and has been named one of fifty, fast-growing, small businesses in St. Louis by *St. Louis Small Business Monthly*.

When Shannon is not saving the world, she is busy at home with her two growing boys and husband. She states that being a contributing author to "Hear Her Now" has been an amazing journey for her. Shannon believes that writing this chapter has been validation of her healing, growth, and strength. She would like to thank her family and friends for all of their love and support through the journey.

Shannon Shores
314-479-2905
shannon@well-ex.com
www.samedaystdtesting.com
fb.me/conductorshores
www.linkedin.com/in/shannon-shores-2a0b5576/

KRISTY BARTON

Hope

Have you ever wanted something so badly in your life you could actually see the vision? The image is faint, like it's burned into your retinas, but you have no idea if or when it will ever happen. I married the Love of My Life more than eight years ago. Doug and I met when we were in our thirties. We knew we wanted to start a family, but we were both old-fashioned, so we waited to start until we got married.

As many of you have probably experienced multiple times in your lifetime, the question of: "When are you and Doug going to have children?" started right away. We even had some people at the wedding reception ask!

In case you didn't know, getting pregnant is not easy. In fact, I have had family and friends who have experienced all kinds of issues before, during, and after pregnancy. I had watched my friends and family go through the good and bad sides of being pregnant. I figured it was just a matter of time.

One year went by. Then two years. Fast forward and we were already at four years of trying to get pregnant. By this point we had done everything we could possibly do and afford. We had spent more than $50,000. We had seen the so-called best-of-the-best specialists, and multiple doctors told us the same thing: "Great news, you and Doug are really healthy; we just cannot figure out why you cannot get pregnant."

We're overachievers. We figured if we did everything and then some, we'd get pregnant. That, my friends, is so **not** the case! In fact, Doug and I are part of those 10 percent of couples that just cannot get pregnant and doctors cannot explain why.

For four years, we hid our pain. We'd end up only sharing our journey with a few family and friends. In the beginning, I think we felt embarrassed, even ashamed. As time went on, we both became very angry. As with most experiences, this is not a cliché unless you've walked in our shoes, you had no idea how painful this was for both of us.

Four years. Four years of hoping, wishing, praying, drinking, and a whole lot of crying. Nothing had changed. We were still just a party of two.

We thought about adoption, but weren't sure if we wanted to go down that path. We weren't sure if we could even afford to try.

At the four-year mark of our marriage, trying to start a family had made us broke, we felt trapped in neutral, and honestly, at this point we weren't sure if we'd ever get to experience the joys of being parents.

Were we always going to be RSVPing only for two? Would driving two SUVs ever see one or maybe two car seats someday? At this point, life sucked!

We had one shot left of becoming parents and adoption seemed to be the right fit for us. In case you're wondering, we did look into hiring a surrogate, but we are two regular people. We couldn't afford that option.

We began to research the hell out of adoption. What are the costs? Will we be able to afford all of the crazy adoption fees? How long will it take to adopt in the U.S.? Would adopting overseas be cheaper and quicker? Are we too old?

Once we figured out what adoption option would be best for us, we began to move forward without a second thought.

About the same time, I also started my own company. Why now? Why not? Life was already super stressful. It was my time to work for someone I loved, myself! I wanted to be able to help area businesses with all their PR/Marketing needs, but most importantly, I wanted the freedom to be able to be with our child whenever that was necessary.

We started the long process of adoption in May 2015.

Unlike during the first four years of our marriage, I began sharing our journey to become parents with many people. To my surprise, we were not alone. Many people opened up about their struggles to become parents. I also discovered a whole new support system.

For many years, I had been very angry at God. She and I have had many heart-to-heart conversions. I joke with people that I have God on speed dial and she always knows how I feel about her.

Fast forward four years, just like dealing with all kinds of doctors, the adoption route wasn't any easier. It's uber expensive. The wait is long, and there are no guarantees.

This July, we came the closest we have been to becoming parents. We were chosen by a birth mom in May to parent her child. Our baby boy was due July 8, 2018.

Everything leading up to the baby's birth was going okay. As we got closer to the arrival of our son, things started getting messy. We were told the birth father was told about the pregnancy, but wanted nothing to do with the baby.

As the days got closer to the baby arriving, we were getting our house ready. I even had my mom come to town early just in case the baby arrived before his due date.

We were all set to drive to across the state to pick up our son. Two days before our son was born, the birth dad appeared and said he was going to raise the boy. Who the hell was this man? Are you really the father? Where have you been?

The next week was the worst week of our lives. We were on the most horrific ride of our journey. The adoption was on. Then it was off. Then there was a slight chance we could still adopt our son.

On Tuesday, July 17, the drama from both birth parents exploded. Our heartache was emotionally and physically painful. The plans for our family died. The birth dad was going to raise the child.

I'm sure by now you're thinking, well, people change their minds. The birth parents have the right to change their minds. The answer is yes, of course the birth parents can change their mind.

Without going into an even longer story, the birth parents lied to us and our adoption agency. I believe they had no plans of giving up their son. The birth mom needed insurance, so our agency helped her get Medicaid. The birth mom kept saying she knew the best thing for her son was to be adopted by Doug and me. She also lied about her health. She had some major issues she never disclosed.

As we were grieving for our son, we received an outpouring of support. The kind words, phone calls, cards, texts, and notes have helped us with our grieving process.

The one thing I wasn't prepared to do was defend us on why we will continue to wait to adopt a baby. Why don't you adopt an older child? Why don't you two become foster parents? There is nothing wrong with either of these two options. The problem I have with this unwarranted advice is that people are not taking into consideration why we want to adopt a baby. We want to be able to bring our child home from the hospital. We want to be part of choosing a name, seeing the first giggle, reading the first book, videotaping those first steps. When it comes to adoption, we have no rights and we really don't get to plan anything. The one constant that we have been holding onto all of these years is that we want to be there at the beginning of our child's life, and for once being able to plan and actually call the shots.

Looking back, I know we dodged a huge bullet. While I would have loved to be writing a chapter about our baby boy, I instead have to share with all of you about the grief we're experiencing as we deal with the death of our dream.

God has a plan. I hate hearing that phrase, but I am trying to embrace the thought. For now, the best I can say is that I have hope. I am fierce! I am stubborn! I am a survivor!

While I am not pleased with the outcome of our most recent adoption attempt, I do know there is a baby for us out there. Somewhere, there's a baby or two who needs to be loved by parents like Doug and me. As we continue to grieve, I will try and remain optimistic. Party of three… I sure hope so sometime sooner rather than later.

Hear Her Now

Kristy Barton was born and raised in southern Wisconsin. In middle school, her family moved out to Cheyenne, Wyoming. She lived out west until she left for college—University of Missouri (Mizzou). She earned her bachelor's degree in broadcast journalism and a minor in history. Mizzou's J-School is still touted as one of the best journalism programs in the country.

Kristy started her journalism career at a young age. While lifeguarding and teaching swimming lessons in both high school and college, Kristy managed the PR/Marketing needs for the Parks and Recreation's Swim Department in Cheyenne. After college, she freelanced for a bit until she landed her dream job in St. Louis, Missouri. She was the PR Director for an area Union for 18 years. While she was working for the Union, she embarked on many adventures. She started an in-house PR Department, staff of one. In the1990s, there was still a stigma in many Unions that women couldn't hold a higher position other than being a secretary. Kristy not only built the PR Department, she also developed and maintained a monthly magazine, created slogans that would eventually become trademarked, and helped raise hundreds of thousands of dollars for numerous charities and organizations.

In January 2015, Kristy embarked on one of her craziest ideas to-date, she started her own business: Sunshine Multimedia Consultants—a full-service PR/Marketing firm. The first year was rough, but by year two,

Kristy was making a name for herself throughout the community. In the last few years, she has won numerous awards including the Webster Groves/ Shrewsbury/ Rock Hill Area Chamber of Commerce Outstanding New Chamber Member, and back-to-back awards from the Small Business Monthly for being one of the Top 20 Best PR Firms in St. Louis.

While her business and home life are going extremely well, the only missing piece is the wait to adopt a child. As they say, that chapter has yet to be written.

Kristy Barton
314-220-5050
Kristy@sunshinemultimediallc.com
Sunshinemultimediallc.com
www.facebook.com/Sunshine-Multimedia-Consultants-LLC

Sharon —

Here's to your Force of Nature!!

[signature]

MARY KAUSCH

Becoming A Force of Nature

During my most formative years, I was taught that I needed an education, so I could always take care of myself. I also learned that the only way to advance my career was to become a supervisor, then manager, director, vice president and eventually, president.

Sound familiar?

When the opportunity knocked, I leapt at becoming the Employee Benefit and Medical Department supervisor for a global appliance manufacturer. I was very excited—I was on my way!

We were a team of fourteen serving thousands of salaried, hourly, and union employees, as well as 10,000 retirees. This was an intense role, especially during union negotiations and benefit renewal time, and when someone did not receive the benefits to which they believed they were entitled. Union stewards regularly pounded on my desk and demanded benefit payment OR ELSE!

Making matters worse, I had a boss who did nothing to support and guide me toward success in my role. Eventually he got demoted and became my peer. Within a few weeks, he began sabotaging my work. This went on for almost five years!

My natural order was being disturbed! I was experiencing a total misalignment with my own nature! And it was creating a dire situation in my life: I was thoroughly stressed; my thoughts and feelings were running rampant; I was getting divorced.... My life was completely and utterly out of control. I was out of alignment with my life. I had lost my power!!

I didn't know what I was going to do, I just knew I had to do something.

I had a yearning—an **unyielding** yearning to learn more about my innate strengths and how to use those strengths consistently to earn my living. I was determined to know more of my own human nature and to help others overcome similar frustration.

In fall 1991, I quit my job. During my exit interview, my boss (the vice president of human resources) told me of his regret; that he had done a poor job of managing my creative side and how this had ultimately hurt the company—and me. All I could think was: "Why didn't you tell me this before?" His comment simply provided more conviction for my yearning.

My quest for knowledge took five months, four states, 30,000 miles, cashing in my 401(k), unconditional focus, lots of helpful people, and tons of initiative, perseverance, and resilience. And you know what? It was totally worth it. I have absolutely no regrets!

Alignment Partnership, a company of HR etc!!, began out of my truck, literally! It started as an answer to my personal frustration of being in the wrong role within Corporate America.

Being a lifelong student of Mother Earth and an avid outdoorswoman, I preserved my 401(k) money by living out of my truck while camping with my dog Mollie. You should have seen the looks on my fellow campers' faces when I would emerge from the campground shower house in a business suit, hose and heels on my way to meet a potential client!

Cell phones had been invented. I trusted this new technology to allow me to make appointments and sell what I knew and, more importantly, to learn as much as possible about what I didn't know. What I *did* know was that I had lots to learn, people to meet and places to go!

Along the way, I learned that when we allow or tolerate being out of alignment with our true nature, letting it go unchecked for lengths of time, our life will not get better.... I learned I needed a vision, one that would nurture my nature, a vision that would allow me to serve others from a place of strength. And I learned that *my true nature would never fail me.*

It was time for me to *stop, search and share.*

When I *stopped* doing, and started be-ing, I was then able to reflect and listen to my internal guide—my GPS. Along the way I realized my innate talents and natural feminine energy already had been speaking loudly and guiding me. I kept stopping and listening more intently with each passing day.

I *searched* for mentors. This was during the height of "experiential learning"—also known as action learning and learning by doing. Being an outdoorswoman and a kinesthetic learner, I was naturally drawn to ropes challenge courses as a training medium. I found several mentors who were generous, knowledgeable, supportive, challenging, and enjoyable. They shaped my future! With their encouragement, my choice of aligning my true nature with my knowledge was completely logical. They taught me about the practical side of people management—that by doing the right things with aligned words and actions, fairness and consistency, and respecting and listening to employees, leaders and managers could provide what's required for employees to be their most productive.

I *shared* what I was learning. I began designing and facilitating experiential training sessions in the great outdoors—it came quickly and easily. I was a natural! Having a solid understanding of employment law and human resource policies and practices, I was compelled to guide managers and leaders in fair and consistent people-management practices. And that's just what I did. During these sessions I observed that people would say one thing yet do something else. This seemed unnatural! I helped managers, leaders, and their teams innately understand, through their behaviors, that *words aligned with actions create trust.* Without this alignment, distrust manifests, creating a downward spiral of morale and performance—another basic law of human nature.

Over the next few years, I learned about group development and process, team formation, motivation, adult learning, training methodologies, organization development and theories, performance coaching, facilitation and, most importantly, the laws of human nature.

Most critical in all of this: I learned about my own true nature and my strengths—something I was able to accomplish with mentors who believed in me. They helped me learn that by aligning the true nature of my strengths with the work that had to be performed, I could consistently surpass expectations, goals, and benchmarks, and ultimately achieve success.

My yearning was sated. Honoring my true nature had allowed me to do activities that left me feeling strong and productive. But now it was time to take all I had learned and go home.

Returning to my roots in St. Louis, Missouri in 1997, even with my newfound insights into human nature, I found myself once again wondering what exactly to do next. Yet, unconditionally, I *knew I had* tons of initiative, perseverance and resilience!

First, I *stopped* doing, and remained be-ing so I could tap into my internal guide.

Second, I *searched* for mentors. And once again, found several who were generous, knowledgeable, supportive, challenging, and enjoyable.

And thirdly, I *shared* expertise with my clients and protégés. I also began the practice of giving back to communities that had supported me when I needed them most. I became president of the Organization Development Network (ODN), the Association for Talent Development (ATD) and the Mid County Chamber of Commerce. I also volunteered to be the membership vice president of the National Speakers Association (NSA).

While I may not have followed the path I was taught during my most formative years, I followed the path of my own true nature. I gained perspectives by stopping to listen to my own GPS, by searching for mentors who saw my potential when I couldn't, and growing my confidence by sharing my experiences and expertise with others.

My roots keep growing. And they keep getting stronger.

To know people, one must understand human nature, and **Mary Kausch** knows *people*—specifically employees and employers. Imagine what could be accomplished if the RIGHT people were given the RIGHT roles and responsibilities so they could make the RIGHT contributions to your organizational goals!

Mary's unique knowledge and powerful insights stem from her lifelong study of human nature and her deeply held belief that every employee is first and foremost, a person—a multi-dimensional human being who exists in a complex organizational ecosystem. Mary offers the *inner insight* needed to align an organization's employee relations, engagement, talent, and education.

Alignment Partnership, a company of HR etc!!, was born out of Mary's frustration with the limitations placed on her by corporate America and a yearning to earn her living doing things that inspired and energized her. After quitting her corporate job in 1991, she set out on a path to help others find fulfillment in their work lives.

As Chief Alignment Officer at Alignment Partnership, Mary is more than well-qualified to address the unique needs of any organization of any size. She has more than thirty years of management and leadership experience. She has a degree in human resources and industrial commu-

Continued...

nications. Before starting her business, she worked in human resources for Health Systems Management, Citicorp, Whirlpool, and the Tecumseh Leadership Center. As an independent organization development consultant, facilitator, and speaker (including DiSC and iWAM certifications and Myers Briggs qualification), Mary knows what it takes to bring each employee's knowledge, skills, and abilities into alignment for maximum effort and contribution.

Mary Kausch
314-409-6622
Mary@AlignmentPartnership.com
www.AlignmentPartnership.com
www.linkedin.com/in/employeerelationsauthority/
www.facebook.com/Alignment-Partnership-1687910611477222/
www.twitter.com/MaryKausch

DEBI CORRIE

Waiting for Success

My mother was an incredible influence in my life. She grew up in a rough middle-class neighborhood. She was married at nineteen and had her first child at twenty. She was a stay-at-home mom until my brother started kindergarten in 1970. That was the year she decided to go back to work. My mother taught me that when you are at work give it your full attention. When you are at home concentrate on your family. She made her schedule work to spend time with us. She chose sitters in the summer that were close to work, so she could take us to lunch on Fridays. She worked close to home in case there was an emergency. She made herself a life she enjoyed.

My mom was a secretary. She excelled at her career, but she wanted more. When we started high school, she went back to college. She wanted to have a career. College was not easy for my mother, but she had a plan and a goal, and she was not going to let anyone, or anything get in her way.

At the age of forty-four she graduated with a four-point-zero GPA and went on to start the second leg of her career. The year was 1986, the same year I graduated from college. We were both off to start a new adventure.

When my mom finished her degree in 1986, she was working at Monsanto and had applied for numerous positions there. No one could see her potential. She had been an administrative assistant or secretary most of her career. Now she had her college degree and was being blocked at every attempt to move up and out of her comfort zone. In 1986, there were not a lot of women in executive roles. None of us expected what she did next!

In the fall of 1986, she came home and told my father that she was going to go to work for MetLife. She was going to work at night for a while and keep her job at Monsanto while she trained. MetLife sold life insurance, annuities, and mutual funds. My mother would no longer have a regular paycheck after training; she would be working on straight commission. My mother had never been in sales or sold anything. We were all in disbelief, and quite frankly didn't think that she would stick with it. We didn't see her vision.

My mother did something amazing. She didn't wait for us to get on board. She saw the potential of this career change and realized that she would be rewarded for her work the same as her male counterparts. She got to work. She learned everything she could about the insurance industry. She studied selling, she believed in her product, and believed that she could do it. She didn't have a Plan B. She saw the potential to help people, make a good living, and be treated as an equal. She chose to pursue this incredibly hard new career that would give her unlimited possibilities. She chose to be accountable for her future, her effort, her successes, and her failures.

It was my first of many adult life lessons I would learn from my mother. By her actions, she showed me anything is possible when you put your mind to it. My mother made the MetLife Leader's Conference every year except for three. The first year she started, the year my parents moved to New Jersey, and the year my parents moved to Milwaukee. She started her business three times in her thirty-year career. My mother taught me that life is full of excuses. My mother didn't try, hope, or wish to be successful. She did the necessary work to make it happen. She designed her own life and her own success.

She taught me that it doesn't matter if there are obstacles. Stop complaining about them. They are only obstacles if you allow them to stop you or get in your way. Sometimes obstacles are your next opportunity.

Three things happened next that I will never forget. Someone recommended that I read "The Confidence Code" by Katty Kay and Claire Shipman. That book changed the way I looked at myself. Before, I had attributed my success to luck, not the hard work I had put in. Men talk about their successes, women tend to wait until someone notices. Men are more likely to negotiate their pay and next employment move. Women rarely negotiate. It really opened my eyes to the fact I had not been managing my own career but waiting for things to happen.

In 2012, I turned fifty—a significant milestone. Suddenly, I was tired of waiting for things to happen. In July 2012, I went to a Mary Kay event. I met Mary Kay National Sales Director Gena Rae Gass. She was a woman who had used direct sales to create a life she loved. If she could do it, I could do it. In August 2012, I started my first direct sales business. For the next three years, I learned how to run a business, while still working a full-time job.

I associated with successful sales people, sales directors, and national sales directors. I built a team. I learned how being around positive people can change your self-talk. What you tell yourself, is what you become. Opportunity doesn't tap you on the shoulder and announce that it is here for you. Sometimes opportunity comes in disguise. You see, I didn't realize that Mary Kay would be the first step in a journey to becoming an entrepreneur.

For the next three years, I had the goal of being a sales director. There was just one problem; I wasn't willing to do the work. I wasn't consistent. I didn't want to be a sales director more than I wanted anything else in the world. How do I know this? When you have the right goal you will do whatever it takes. You see, unless you are all in, like my mother, your goals just won't work. Sometimes when you have the wrong goal, another opportunity presents itself.

While I was running my Mary Kay business, I met Kris Rosser. She was testing products, and I asked her what she would do if she could do anything in the world. Much to my surprise she said she would do taxes and sell real estate. "Seriously?" I asked. "I am a CPA and would love to do taxes, too," I told her.

A year later our tax company would be formed. We wanted to focus on solo entrepreneurs and single owner LLCs. We not only remain strong business partners, but best friends today. We share a passion to help small business owners be successful.

By October 2015, I realized my dream had changed. I had transformed several of my Mary Kay friends into my first tax clients. My original dream of being a Mary Kay sales director was no longer what I wanted. Most importantly, it taught me that it is okay for dreams to evolve and change.

By August 2016, I did something I never thought I would. I jumped off the W-2 bandwagon and become a partner at B2B CFO®, the largest CFO firm in the United States. I was going to be a business owner. This was a serious commitment without a safety net. As a business owner, I was responsible for finding my own clients. No one would be sending me a paycheck—I would be earning my own fees. My husband, our friends, and my family thought I had lost my mind. You see, I knew something that they didn't. I was all in. I loved this work and I was good at it. I loved helping people be successful. These were all lessons my first business Mary Kay had taught me.

If you are in a service industry, you must like people. You must connect with like-minded people. You truly do make your own success and you must be passionate about what you do. Every day, I get to live the life I have created for myself. You see, I now have time for volunteer work, to serve on a nonprofit board, and to speak in public. My new career allows me to pursue my goal of education for children, soon to be entrepreneurs, and business owners. It has allowed me the freedom to decide how I spend my time and reap the benefits of my efforts.

My mother taught me to get rid of the excuses. Stop telling yourself what you can't do, but what you can do. Figure out your rocks, like my mother did, and move them out of your way. Better yet, go beyond them and just pursue your dream! No one can make it happen except for you. Do something to move your business forward every day. When you set a goal, do it. When you make a promise, keep it. Be willing to do the things necessary to make you successful. Be a lifelong learner: listen to podcasts, watch TED talks, read books, talk to people in and out of your industry, and keep yourself open to new opportunities. Figure out what success means to you. Only you can create the life you want, and only you can make your dreams come true.

Debi Corrie is a business owner and partner at B2B CFO®. Debi is a financial professional with thirty years of experience. As a forward thinker, Debi helps business owners concentrate on the future.

In addition to B2B CFO, she owns two other businesses to help others learn how to create their own brand of success through education, coaching, and writing.

Debi received her bachelor of science degree in business administration with a major in accounting from the University of St Louis while working full-time. She is a certified public accountant, CGMA and a member of the American Institute of Certified Public Accountants (AICPA) and the National Association of Tax Professionals (NATP). She is a Vistage Trusted Advisor, mentor for Parkway Spark, board member for the Professional Women's Alliance of St Louis, board member for Inventors Association of St. Louis, and chair of the Inner Circle of Springfield.

She has taught classes on financing startups and business economics for the Veteran's Business Resource Center in St Louis and SBDC in Illinois. She speaks publicly on a variety of topics to educate people about how to use numbers to make their future business endeavors successful and to analyze risks.

She has dedicated this chapter to her mother Georgia Robedeau, Gena Rae Gass, and Kris Rosser Schmitt.

Debi Corrie
618-541-1197
debi@djc-media.com
www.djc-media.com
twitter.com/djc-media

DJC Media, LLC
540 Regency Centre
Collinsville, IL 62234

PAM WILSON

Freedom

My life as I knew it changed forever the day I decided I was worth it. The day I decided that my light, my voice needed to shine in any and all ways.

This day didn't come without much careful thought, consideration and discussion. Not to mention tears of frustration, joy and sadness.

This is a story of a woman who finally understood, "Those that bring sunshine to the lives of others cannot keep it from themselves." This is a story about a story-teller. This is a story about understanding how to suit up. This is a story about taking the high road. Even if it meant I was on the high road ALONE most of the time.

This is a story about a Warrior who is going to make it after all.

I paid a huge price for my freedom. Freedom from a life and a marriage that were not healthy for anyone involved including the children in the house and certainly not for me. My marriage had turned into a battleground years prior. As smart as I am, as creative as I am, as optimistic as I am, I was like the proverbial frog that was living in tepid water. When the water boiled it was too late-I was gone.

My voice, my sunshine, my light.

All of it simply gone. I had no idea how bad I felt all the time, the unhealthy environment I continued to stay in. People often ask why I stayed as long as I did. We all have our reasons for doing certain things.

This was not one of my better ideas.

When the staying became impossible, when life became so very dark, it was time to go. I could barely breathe anymore.

It's been a long legal battle which I never wanted, never wanted to fight or participate with. And yet, like the last years of my marriage, I found myself in a situation that required Warrior-like skill to survive. After years of being bullied and diminished, I learned how to battle well. I found like-minded Warriors who helped me in every capacity understand the battle ground I was standing on and coming out of. I had an idea that there was strength deep within and I could and would access it over the course of two long years. It wasn't always pretty.

And yet, my voice which I heard each time I responded to questions by lawyers, judges, friends, acquaintances didn't sound like my voice at all.

Until one day it suddenly did. The change was gradual…and yet, I felt my voice growing stronger. It surprised me as much as anyone.

Would I change things given the opportunity? Knowing what I know now absolutely-in a New York minute. I would change so many things about this past life-and I would start back at the beginning. It's taken me a long time to discern why I stopped fighting for myself. Why I backed down. And what I found is that after years and years of constantly being treated poorly and then even worse, I just surrendered.

It was easier.

I had no fight left in me.

Until I did.

And let me tell you, after those first shell-shocked months of constant surprises I found my soul, my fight, my light.

My sister who witnessed most of this constantly shakes her head in disbelief. "This is YOU. This person. You've changed so much and for the better. Outside of that environment you're a completely different person."

I paid a huge price for my freedom.

I paid a huge price for my voice.

Yet, I know from responses and insight from family, friends and other Warriors, this ME, this VOICE is the real me. The authentic me. Often, I am reminded by circumstance what my authentic voice sounds like. It's love. It's honesty. It's standing my ground in a completely understandable, acceptable, and yes, freeing way. It's putting positive energy into the world as often as I possibly can. In any way.

So, with my new found freedom and my voice I look at this new life I've been creating. It's scary, exciting, fun, worrisome, anxiety-ridden, and full of adventure-its life. I made the choice and yet, here I sit at Freedoms' Door and I can't make sense of it. It's too big, too awkward, and too hard to get my arms around.

I'm having a hard time embracing what IS, what it finally feels like to be able to breathe, make my own choices, makes mistakes and learn from them. I'm having a hard time looking at all this freedom as…fun.

Yes, I understand all of life is not fun. I get it.

On the other hand, why can't it be? I've always wondered what it would be like to have a vacation mind-set all the time. Easy, breezy, relaxed. I have this feeling I might not have been created quite this way.

Over the past few years I've continued practicing yoga and keeping an open mind when I hear, "Live in the moment." Or, "Take care of you. Support yourself. Be gentle, kind, compassionate." "Take what you need, leave what you don't." Ah, compassion, my old friend. We are all much more compassionate to others than we are to ourselves. I'm slowly learning how to be gentle, kind and accepting of me and my voice.

Okay, I certainly left what I didn't need. And I took with me and continue each and every day to think about what I need and what I want. Sometimes I get so tired of thinking. When does it all just happen?!

I paid a huge price for my freedom.

As my ever-evolving journey continues I've been listening more actively and intuitively to the messages the Universe has been sending. Within two days the following quote made its way to me, "Anxiety is like praying for what I don't want." Always one to default to optimism and sunshine, I've changed my thinking…yes, I still worry and yes, there is often a low-level anxiety, however, I'm trying to remember that RIGHT NOW I am okay. Right now this very minute. And if I'm not, the last two years have shown me that I will figure it out. There might be tears and sadness, AND I will figure it out.

My vision for life comes from my oft-asked question: What makes a life? For me, it's those small moments of everyday life. Looking at a gorgeous sunrise, tracking the glittering planets at night in a star-filled sky, being with those I trust and love, family. Being. Just being. Breathing and letting things BE. Again, giving myself permission to explore, investigate, smile, love and…BE.

I paid a huge price for my freedom. I finally understood that in order to free my voice and free myself, this was the choice that had to be made. I'm a better person for it, hopefully inspiring others through my writing and my work. Gradually by finding my voice again through my freedom my purpose becomes clearer.

My life as I knew it changed forever the day I decided I was worth it. The day I decided that my light, my voice needed to shine in any and all ways.

Freedom

Pam Wilson is a writer, licensed Master Social Worker, Book Coach and creator/facilitator of Write ON! a community-based writing program that empowers participants to find their voice and inspire change in the world. See the work at: https://www.facebook.com/WriteONstlouis/ This program has been successfully implemented in middle school, high school, home-school and community groups.

Pam recently began work as the Writing Instructor for the Cancer Support Community of St. Louis.

Her Book Coaching with Davis Creative began in January 2017; she has successfully coached authors to publication. She is also the Editor of the INNERgized Anthology published in October 2017 as well as this anthology.

For fifteen years she wrote the S.O.S. From Suburbia column for "St. Louis Moms and Dads," part of the St. Louis Post-Dispatch. The columns were about real life written in a relatable, humorous way. Find them at: http://www.stltoday. com/lifestyles/parenting. She has written free-lance pieces that appeared in St. Louis Magazine/Family edition both on-line and in print. She has written the "Off the Beaten Path" column for Swim-BikeRun St. Louis chronicling her adventures in out of the ordinary exercise options.

Continued…

In 2012, she self-published SOS from Suburbia, a compilation of humorous essays which supported her belief that a well-told, entertaining story about individuality and family was welcome and needed in our common community. She put the real back into reality with commentary on everyday life. Presently, she writes a blog about her oh-so-interesting life where she puts her unique spin on everyday happenings and the journey of being human at: https://youcallitchaosicallitlife.wordpress.com

Pam has raised two amazing kids over the last twenty years. She loves to bike, read, travel, dance and hike with her dog. One day she hopes to live on or near a beach. Previously she was a school social worker in the Special School District of St. Louis after earning a Masters of Social Work from Washington University. Her undergraduate degree is in Child and Family development from University of Missouri at Columbia.

Pam Wilson
groovychickpjw@gmail.com
pam@daviscreative.com
www.stltoday.com/lifestyles/parenting
youcallitchaosicallitlife.wordpress.com
www.facebook.com/WriteONstlouis/
www.stltoday.com/lifestyles/parenting
www.linkedin.com/in/pam-wilson-14477110a/

LISA BOBYAK

The Three Lies that Kept me from Living the Life I was Designed for

She walked into the coffee shop and she looked adorable. Wearing a fabulous denim jacket with cute boho jewelry, it was clear that she'd taken time to style her hair into loose beachy waves.

My client pulled off her polished look with skinny jeans and trendy boots effortlessly.

On the outside she was completely pulled together.

Yet, once she got her coffee and settled in for our coaching session, the truth came out.

"The truth is, on the inside, I'm drained and feel like I'm running on empty," she said.

I wonder if you can relate to my client.

I sure can, because I can remember when I WAS my client.

On the outside, life looks balanced and beautiful.

But on the inside, there's a driving and striving that leaves us feeling exhausted and unfulfilled.

In our "do more to be more" culture, it's hard to find the exit off this hamster wheel.

My client asked, "So, what IS the answer to stop running on empty, so I can love my life again?"

In short, here's what I told her:

You've got to stop believing the lies and put yourself first.

I know, it sounds a bit selfish.

I get it. As a high achiever myself, for most of my life putting myself first was the last thing on my list.

I'm a pastor's kid and I grew up in a bucolic small community in Pennsylvania. I raised two daughters and I'm now running a coaching, consulting, and speaking business.

As I look back on my life, I can see where the lies I once believed kept me stuck on autopilot for years and kept me from living the life I was designed for.

In the work I do, I see those same lies keeping my clients trapped on that hamster wheel, working hard to get what they want, yet never feeling fulfilled.

Knowing these lies I once believed can smooth the path toward living the life you've been designed for.

Growing up in rural Lancaster County Pennsylvania, I was surrounded by well-meaning neighbors and church members. Because I was the pastor's daughter, they all kept an eye out for me.

Mostly loving and curious, the members of the church watched me grow up from the time I was a baby to a teenager. It was like living in a beautiful, yet publicly displayed fishbowl.

Even though my community meant no harm, the result was that I grew up feeling watched, scrutinized, and judged, and it tainted the way I perceived everything going forward.

Sadly, I couldn't shake the feeling of being on display and open to criticism until I was well into my forties… more than twenty years past being known as a Pastor's Kid.

I didn't think it was a big deal.

But, its impact leads to Lie Number One.

Lie Number One: It's always good to put others first.

Up until my mid-forties, my internal dialogue was focused on what other people were thinking; about how I could help them and make their life better.

It was routine for me to consider others before myself.

I was the fixer, the easygoing one, the one who would acommodate for the good of the group.

I learned that it was selfish to take care of myself.

So, I didn't.

And, because my thoughts and energy were focused on how to please others, I didn't learn how to please myself.

Each one of us has been divinely created with unique gifts.

I now believe that it's our responsibility to learn what those gifts are and to share them with the world.

When our attention is focused on feeling judged; when our energy is drained by our constant striving to prove our worth . . . we can't fully engage in the life we're meant to live.

Sadly, in our effort to prove ourselves, many high-achieving women are unknowingly running away from what they've been designed to do.

You've been purposely designed, and it's your responsibility to take care of yourself so you can live the life you were created for.

Truth Number One: It's your responsibility to respect yourself like you do others.

I married my college sweetheart just two months after graduating. Because his industry was going through major transitions, we moved nine times in the first six years of our marriage. During these moves, as a new teacher, I was hired and then had to let go of four different teaching positions. And I enrolled into three post-graduate programs. During this time, our two daughters were born.

I always had dreams of becoming a school principal, and yet after my girls were born, I felt compelled to stay at home and raise them.

I told myself that after things settled down and the girls were a bit older, I would go back and get my master's degree and become a principal.

Which leads to Lie Number Two.

Lie Number Two: I can do it later.

Later didn't come, and sadly, neither did my master's degree.

Life moved at a clip and I pushed aside what I gave up.

The girls were active and had many interests.

To keep my hands involved in teaching, I volunteered at church and in the girls' schools.

I managed to keep my husband organized and poised for the next promotion.

My schedule was too full for me to work out. I was too busy to eat well. There was too much to do for me to head to bed at a decent time . . . .

Consequently, my weight and blood pressure crept up. "Once our life is more settled and I have more time, I'll get on the list. I can take care of myself later," I said.

In response to an unrelated medical scan, I was sent to a neurosurgeon's office. I was too busy to make the appointment, so they made it for me.

I figured this was just precaution, and I was impatient as I waited on the cold, paper-covered exam table. Thoughts ran through my head, "I need to get home to run the girls to their evening lessons. I really don't have time for this."

The doctor eventually came into the room and her voice was stern as she said, "You've had a stroke." She pulled out the X-rays and revealed the dead spot on my brain.

The doctor's tone switched from stern to annoyed, as she noticed my agitated demeanor. *(I didn't have time for this, remember? I still thought that it was all precautionary.)*

"I can't tell you how many women I see who are just like you. You're too busy to take care of yourself. You think that you've got all the time in the world to take your health seriously. But I'm telling you, if you don't take care of yourself now, you won't have another chance."

Truth Number Two: Act now, so you can enjoy your life later.

That office visit was my wake-up call, and I began to take my health seriously.

I ate better and moved more. With my healthier food choices and more physical activity, my body slept well at night and my life felt pretty good.

Until… my husband said that he wanted "to talk."

"The talk" lasted less than twenty minutes.

And in that time, he confessed his three-year affair and told me that he wanted a divorce.

With no regard to his complete insensitivity, he tossed an attorney's business card onto the coffee table in front of me and said, "I know you don't believe in affairs, so you'll want a divorce. Here's a lawyer's card. He's expecting your call."

My world, as I knew it, was over.

Who was I if I wasn't a wife? I'd had that role for twenty years.

And that reality leads to Lie Number Three.

Lie Number Three: My value is determined by my roles.

I've been told that only five percent of divorces end up going to trial. Most get settled out-of-court.

Ours didn't.

Because I wasn't bringing money into the family, the court needed to determine what I was worth.

After many assessments, aptitude tests, intelligence tests, vocational assessments, every one of them humiliating and dehumanizing, my worth was determined.

I was valued at $32,000 a year.

It was degrading.

Yet, as awful as this experience was, I never did believe this lie. I believed the truth.

Truth Number Three: No one determines my value. I'm more precious than jewels.

I was raised by parents who told me that I was a daughter of God, and my worth is in my Father's eyes. No person or job title could determine my worth.

And yet, even with that strong foundation, my self-worth took a huge hit during our two-plus year, litigious divorce and the ensuing seven-year process to enforce the judgment.

I was surrounded by messages that went against what I believed to be true.

Written in countless documents, spoken out loud in my private "rehabilitation sessions," talked about openly around the large mediation table, and ruled upon in the courtroom.

"Ms. Bobyak is worth $32,000 a year."

For me to move forward, and to live the life that I was designed for, I needed to stop believing the lies.

And so, my journey began.

Over time, I considered my needs and wants in every decision I made.

Rather than waiting for a later time, I began to act on things that were important to me.

The Three Lies that Kept me from Living the Life I was Designed for

And I began to understand the true value of being a cherished daughter of God.

Because I was able to catch the lies I once believed, I was also able to find my truths.

I no longer strive to please others, yet because I'm living the life I was created for other people are indeed served.

I now help high-achieving women connect to the important work they've been designed for, without losing themselves in the process.

In essence, I help them stop running on empty, so they can love their lives again.

I wonder if you have something in common with the beautiful, polished client I met at the coffee shop?

Could there be lies that you believe, that are keeping you from aligning your outside with your inside?

You've been designed for a purpose.

Hop off the hamster wheel with me.

Stop believing the lies.

And, begin to love the life you've been designed for.

Lisa Bobyak, founder of Living Fully Balanced, LLC, has become the go-to source for balance and life design in Minneapolis. She is dedicated to working with high-achieving women and organizations to increase their energy and focus. These women know that they've been designed to make an impact on their world, and they don't want to lose themselves in the process. Lisa's been transforming women's lives for more than fourteen years through her inspirational and educational presentations as well as her private coaching. However, she's best known for her proven signature program, "Love Your Life Again." Lisa is the author of *7 Days to Loving Your Life Again*. Because she's overcome unexpected challenges and thrived in spite of them, it's become her mission to support women as they make their impact on the world.

Lisa F. Bobyak
612-702-9848
lisa@livingfullybalanced.com
www.livingfullybalanced.com/
www.linkedin.com/in/lisabobyak/
www.facebook.com/livingfullybalanced/
www.facebook.com/lisa.bobyak
www.youtube.com/channel/UCrwrHQzeGIjl0180ezXfy7A

SANDY TOMEY

The Power of the Sacred Love Journey

I talked with my beloved deceased husband yesterday. He passed over into Spirit about eight months ago. While I've talked with him every single day since then, yesterday he talked back. I had a long-anticipated session with an evidential medium, and it was wonderful to have even more confirmation of what I had always known in my heart and soul: Spirit lives on and we are always connected to those we love.

No one ever wants to hear at fifty-two years old, or at any age, the words, *triple hit* non-Hodgkin's lymphoma. What? Was just the regular kind not enough? Did it really have to be triple hit? It was an extremely rare type of cancer with a very poor prognosis. With those few words, life as we knew had ended, and a new chapter in our sacred love journey had begun. We had just experienced eight of the most glorious years of my life; deeply in love, passionate about our calling, and traveling to our favorite national parks, beaches, and jungles. All the while sharing our gifts with others and committed to making the world a better place. The depth of love we shared with each other and our families was profound. After this diagnosis, we had eight months of fighting for his life, paralysis and pain, accepting death, and deeply understanding the true meaning of our vows… in sickness and in health.

Steve and I met on a dating site in the spring of 2010. The journey to finding one another was a long and sacred one. I had recently ended a sixteen-year marriage and he had been a single dad for many years. After years of living my life only in Mom-mode, and not being fulfilled in many parts of my life, I set out on a journey of self-discovery and committed to doing whatever it took to live my best life. It was that journey that led me to deeply loving myself, and eventually to understanding how my attitudes and beliefs were creating everything in my life, both the good and the not-so-good. Being willing to look within and observe the thoughts I took for granted and the beliefs that were limiting me truly transformed my world.

One of the beliefs that I discovered that kept me stuck for many years was my viewpoint on divorce. The old belief that disempowered me was Divorce = Failure. Thoughts of "I am not good enough," "Nobody loves me," "What did I do wrong," and "Why is this happening to me" plagued me and kept me stuck.

Once I became aware of this and made the choice to change my thoughts, my experience of life also transformed. I decided to choose the empowering viewpoint: "Look how wise and powerful I am to endure a difficult time, learn and grow through it, and have the wisdom to know better what I want the second time around and the courage to go after it."

It was that empowering story that I chose to tell myself and believe INSTEAD OF the disempowering one that led me to successfully finding Steve, the love of my life.

It was through using the incredible power of positive thought that I manifested Steve. Manifested him? Yes, I did. I put an order out to the Universe for a man with all the qualities I wanted. I learned from my past mistakes, did my own deep work on self-love, and knew exactly what I was looking for and knew that I would not settle for anything less than what my heart and soul desired. I added a very important caveat at the end: "This or something EVEN BETTER!" In all the important ways, Steve was everything I asked for. And in ways I did not yet have the awareness about to ask specifically for, he was EVEN BETTER. We aligned in our core values of family, service, faith, and desire to make the world a better place while raising the consciousness of the planet. We both loved to travel and go on adventures, and boy did we! We were true spiritual partners and we looked forward to travelling even more together, teaching and coaching together, and continuing to make the world a better place. The story I believed, that I was worthy of an amazing, loving man, and my confidence and commitment to finding him were the secret sauce that attracted us to each other.

We were crushed and disappointed when we heard the diagnosis, and slowly the realization of the journey ahead of us crept in. We survived those eight months by honoring our love, being present, and living each and every moment to the fullest. Our family love and support played a vital role during that time. And now, with Steve having transitioned back to Spirit, I am left once again with a CHOICE on the story I choose to tell myself about these events and what they mean. My feelings are important, but they don't have anything to do with the story I tell myself and what I make these events mean. What I am feeling is sad and disappointed. I feel lonely and sad that my best friend and lover is no longer in physical form. And even a little bit angry that just as life was getting good, he is gone. I also feel grateful—for the amazing years we had together and for the learning and growth that can only come as you walk with your beloved along the final days transitioning from this physical form back to spirit. Finally, I feel blessed that I got to spend the few years that I did with such an amazing and vibrant soul.

The power I hold in my hands NOW is THE STORY I tell myself around these events. The facts are that he died; he loved deeply and was loved by many. His physical presence is no longer here. The STORY I tell myself around that is where all the power lies—both empowering or disempowering—and it is up to me to decide WHICH story I want to believe.

I know that if I tell myself a story that this is awful, that he died too young, that he did not deserve it, that I did not deserve it, or his family did not deserve it, that story disempowers me and keeps me stuck in the sadness, negativity, and grief. I know I cannot live my purpose in that energy and it would certainly not honor Steve to stay there.

Another story that is just as true: the purpose of each of our lives is to share our gifts and passions with the world and make our little corner of it a better place. Steve did that better than almost anyone I know. In ALL fifty-two years of his life! The ripples of his inspiration live on in the thousands of students he taught. His "students" were ready to lead, so it was time for him to pass, because his purpose was complete. He taught his family everything he could while living, so the other things we might still need to learn could only be learned by his passing and the journey we each will take in our grief and understanding and learning to accept it.

Neither one of these stories are ultimate Truth. Both are opinions and choices on what we want to believe. I know the feelings I will have when I believe each of these thoughts. The first story disempowers me and when I think that thought, I feel sad and my body feels heavy and toxic. I know if I allow myself to believe the first story for any length of time, I will never be able to create the life I am called to create. It would keep me stuck, feeling sad and mad. I certainly have times throughout the day that this choice feels very appealing and I surely go there from time-to-time.

The second story is the one I choose to believe. I do realize it has taken me a lifetime of learning and growth to truly believe this second story. This story not only empowers me but takes something that could be devastating and transforms it into beauty and light! This story does not dismiss my feelings—I still feel all of them—but believing this second story lessens the time I spend there and gives me so much more time to live my life in a way that Steve would want me to.

In the end, Steve did have a message for us from the evidential medium. He shared with us that the physical pain in his body was too much to

The Power of the Sacred Love Journey

bear. Because of that and the full life he lived, he was ready to go, and he acknowledged to us how helpful it was to him during his last days that we were able to let him go with grace and love. He reminded us how we were all together during that time and family bonding happened even more fully because of that sacred experience when he passed over to Spirit. What most of us think as the worst time ever, suddenly became a sacred and deeply powerful experience.

The final story I choose to believe is that *everything is sacred*. When we can start to view every experience not so much in terms of good, bad, right, or wrong, but rather, ALL OF IT as experiences along the Sacred Journey of life that make us who we are, perhaps suffering can be relieved. Perhaps that is where our real power lies… knowing that each and every moment, we are right where we need to be on our sacred journey. That by being human and in physical form, we get to CHOOSE what stories we want to believe and how we want to spend these very precious and few years we each have in the physical world. For me, I will always choose love.

Sandy Tomey is owner and founder of Sacred Journeys Enterprises, a coaching and retreat company that specializes in helping women heal their heart and reconnect to their passion and purpose so they can create a life they love with the with the love of their life by their side! She is a certified relationship coach for singles and couples with more than eight years of experience in empowering women to be Love Leaders and manifest true and lasting love in their lives.

Sandy has coached hundreds of single and searching women to love themselves so they can attract and marry their soulmates! Her two programs, ***Being "The One": Foundations of Self-Love***, and ***Attracting "The One": Principles of Conscious Dating*** have transformed the lives of lonely singles into fulfilling and thriving partnerships! She leads transformational and inspirational destination retreats in Costa Rica, Florida, Sedona, and along the many rivers of the Missouri Ozarks.

In addition to being a certified relationship coach for both singles and couples, Sandy has a Ph.D. in love and life experiences! Through her own sacred journey through divorce, manifesting her soulmate then losing him to cancer, she knows firsthand both the struggles and joys of dating, marriage, and relationship in every decade of her life. The process she used to heal her own heart, fall in love with herself, manifest genuine love and maintain that love through sorrow and loss is the success formula for her individual and group programs and retreats.

Sandy is a certified relationship coach for both singles and couples, Energy Leadership Master Practitioner, licensed massage therapist and energy healer. She holds her PCC certification through the International Coach Federation and serves on the Leadership Team for the ICF St. Louis chapter.

Are you single and searching or dating and discouraged? Take the next step now on your sacred love journey by taking the Relationship Readiness Quiz:
www.SandyTomey.com or email Sandy@Sandytomey.com

Sandy Tomey
314-322-5052
Sandy@Sandytomey.com
www.SandyTomey.com
www.facebook.com/TheLoveLuminary/
www.linkedin.com/in/sandy-tomey-pcc-1481b98/

GINA NICOLE BALLARD

Guiding Angels and Embracing Your Intuition

It was three fifty-five in the morning, and I was fast asleep and cozied up in my family's cabin in Arroyo Seco Hills, California. The house was completely silent, my Papa was snoring in the room across from me, and the alarm clock began screaming out of nowhere. My tummy churned as it scared me to bits! I got up, hastily turned on the bedside lamp, made sure the alarm was turned to the off position, and returned to sleep.

An hour later at four fifty-five, it blasted again! Heart racing, this time I decided to not take any chances. I pulled the cord out of the wall. I thought for sure that would have done the trick.

That is until one hour later. Five fifty-five a.m., again the buzzer screamed at me. Halfway remembering I had unplugged the clock, I shot up in a panicked confusion. That is when I saw her standing there before me. A figure that I initially thought was my cousin, Kristi.

She didn't respond, nor even move for that matter.

I attempted to ask again, "What are you…." After I was able to speak those three words, I realized I wasn't speaking to Kristi and stopped mid-sentence. My spine shifted upward and sat upright in amusement. I could feel tingles throughout my body. I felt as if someone was staring at me even though this figure was peering outward.

I heard in my outer ear, "I am always watching." At that moment, the figure disappeared literally into thin air.

I remember feeling panicked from the shocking sound of the alarm, and at the same time was calm. I lay back down and took it all in. I almost couldn't believe my eyes. I had seen other figures and outlines in my childhood, but never anything this defined. The figure appeared so real. So vibrant. So human. I took a moment to scan the visit in my mind. I then realized that her clothes were out-of-date, and she really didn't move that much.

I shared the story with my family when everyone got up several hours later.

To this day, I can't be sure if she was an archangel, spirit guide, or guardian angel. It was all so new to me, and I wasn't prepared to move through such visitations as I am now. From meditating with the memory, I believe that she was my Spirit guide, letting me know that she was always going to look out for me.

At that time in my life I was so unclear. I had been praying a lot and giving thanks for the affirmation that I was on the right path. I had also been learning how to deepen my intuition. In response, I kept seeing the number five everywhere, which I didn't understand at the time. Now, I have a language with my spirit team, which you can say is an agreed upon language of sorts. I have various colors, numbers, words, and signs that I know mean certain things. I refer to this as "spirit vocabulary." It is something that I have built over time, by experiencing incidents just as this one, and by practicing through dedication, meditation, and journaling.

Today, I am confident what five means for me: transformation, change, and changing direction. If you put a five on its side, notice how it looks like a table and chairs. Its message: put it all out on the table.

And then there is the alarm. A bold sound that is meant to guide someone to wake up.

Guiding Angels and Embracing Your Intuition

Looking back, I believe this gentle spirit was hinting at all the above. To nudge me and guide me, to put it all out on the table, to embrace transformation, probably shift my direction a bit, *and* let me know I was being watched over (her peering out the door).

Your angels and guides can help you act on new ideas, find romance, resolve arguments, live your purpose, and guide you to your absolute best life possible. If you communicate with them through breath and gratitude, if you trust, and listen, your life *will* transform.

I have been guided to jobs, homes, and resolutions with the help of my angels.

If you doubt angelic or Spirit presence, know their communication can be subtle, and they show up in many ways. It's not every day or all the time that an alarm clock goes off every fifty-five minutes, and angels and guides appear in full form. While that can happen, it can also happen in several other ways.

I am sure you know what it is like to have a gut feeling, or you have caught yourself saying "I knew you were going to say that" to someone. Maybe you experience vivid visuals as you are meditating, hear words, or feel temperature changes or tingles.

You are intuitive, as is everyone. Embrace your inner voice and allow it to grow. It is through your intuition that angels and guides connect with you. They do so in six primary ways, which I refer to as "The 'S' Factors":

1. SAVOR
2. SCENT
3. SENSATION
4. ~~SITE~~ SIGHT
5. SOUND
6. SUGGESTION

Generally speaking, one will be strongest for you, but you can develop them all if you wish. When you understand what you relate to most, you can continue to develop your communication with Spirit.

To briefly touch on each, Savor is to taste, and it is also known as clairgustance. I do this a lot with carrot cake. It's one of my favorite desserts. When I see it on a menu I try to tune in and imagine the taste. I can typically know if it will be moist, sweet, or dry. Spirit may also connect with you by giving you a taste of something in your mouth that reminds you of a loved one, or maybe even gives you a hint to an inquiry you have been having.

The gift of scent is actual smelling, and referred to as clairscent. This can happen in various ways. There are times when I will actually smell spices in our home that are not really there, and I know that Archangel Metatron is hanging out with us. Then there are times when I may smell someone smoking a cigar and it reminds me of my Grandpa. Both are examples of scent.

Sensation is physically feeling and is also known as clairsentience. When I was first diving into building communication with my angels, I had a lot of body work done. I clearly remember one key moment where I felt four hands on my body, when only one woman was working on me. I have also experienced moments where I have a sensation in my body where I can feel a shift in energy, just as I shared earlier, I could feel tingles and a presence. Finally, clairsentience can also be where someone physically pokes you or bumps into you, leading to a next step. I say this is being "nudged" by your angels.

Sight Site is seeing and is also known as clairvoyance. The experience I shared is the perfect example of clairvoyance in many ways. For one, I physically saw a full figure spirit with my naked eye. Two, seeing the number fifty-five repeated time and time again, also held meaning to me. Another way to experience clairvoyance is to see something in your mind's eye, almost like imagining it when your eyes are closed.

Receiving messages through sound or hearing is also known as clairaudience. The alarm clock going off is an example of this. I physically heard with my outer ear the alarm which caught my attention. While I heard that, I also experienced angel whispers in hearing, "I am always watching." Both are examples of sound.

Finally, suggestion or thought, also known as **claircognizance**, is another, and very common way spirit delivers information. As I said, we all have a primary way our teams speak to us. This is definitely my primary way, and I find that people drawn to my work are also "suggestion" or **claircognizance** based. You know, and you don't know how you know. You just know!

If you are wanting to embrace your angels and spirit into your life, bring your awareness to how things may feel, seem, sound, or if you have an inner knowing. This is how they connect to us.

Allow your mind to be free, and always keep the F.A.I.T.H. = Finding Angels In The Heart.

Gina Nicole Ballard is the author and illustrator of the "RYEE Wisdom Cards: Feng Shui With Your Angels." As a Feng Shui practitioner and Certified Intuitive Counselor, she is dedicated to helping people align with their highest purpose and live a spirit-driven life.

Gina began spirit-seeking when she was fifteen years old, diving into crystals, esoteric rituals, and religion—digging for information on the more she knew was out there. From the time she was five, she said she wanted to be a nurse. Even though she knew she disliked blood and could physically feel other people's wounds. She simply knew her truth was to help others live an improved life and didn't know what to call it. After overcoming her own personal challenges in the areas of health, career, and relationships, she has dedicated her life to help others do the same.

Gina is committed to working in a place of light, love, and integrity. Her intention is to remain sincere and have fun, while supporting others with the desire to live an enriched life.

Gina graduated with a master's degree from California State University of Sacramento. She was trained as a Feng Shui practitioner at the BTB School of Feng Shui and certified through the Feng Shui Interior Design program at the New York Institute of Art and Design.

Gina Nicole, LLC
650-284-88070
support@ginanicole.net
www.ginanicole.net
www.facebook.com/visionwithginanicole
www.instagram.com/gina_nicole_b/
www.linkedin.com/in/gina-nicole-ballard-429b759/

DR. HEIDI BROCKE

Feel the Freedom

Earlier this year, I was working on the re-launch of "Coaching with Dr. Heidi," my practice which includes Toxic Relationship Awareness and Healing. The first time I launched I was more or less winging it, but three years later it is proven itself over and over that the mission that chose me is one of a greater importance than I, myself, could ever be.

I needed a word, a word that told people what I do, a word so powerful that people would know they needed my program just by seeing the logo. I wanted something symbolic, but I was coming up blank. I could come up with nothing strong enough to communicate what I needed to say, what I wanted others to see. That is when I began reading the testimonials that had been collected from my program graduates.

Ta-da! Of course! Ask those people I had worked with and talked with for "the word." I sent out as many texts as I could to clients that had completed any or all of my programs. "Give me one word that you would use to describe your life now that you would not have used to describe your life prior to working with me." Of all the people who texted me back, the word "Freedom" was attached to seventy percent of the responses, followed by relief, confidence, happiness, and peace.

FREEDOM!

That was it! Wow! I gave these people freedom? I could hardly believe that I had made such an impact on these lives. After all, I'm just someone who tells my story, makes suggestions, and provides support where needed. People are saying I gave them their freedom back—that is something I never would have expected to hear. Turns out I'm more than just someone who "tells my story."

That day I went into reflection mode…. When I was in the heat of one of several relationships that was not healthy for me, I would have given almost anything to feel free. Just one day of relief, one day of laughter, one day of calm, one day of approval and being good enough. But I remember seldom getting it. Until, of course, one day when that one person walked into my life, giving me the support I needed which allowed me my chance to feel freedom. Thinking back, I feel I owe my life to him, through his experience and support I was able to "get my freedom back.".

Is that how people were feeling about me? If my past was meant to help others feel the way I did in the first few months of my freedom, then I accept my past as my new purpose. I realized that day that my past had turned into my passion, and my life and perspective has changed dramatically.

Working as a full time Toxic Relationship Awareness and Healing Specialist, I use my past experiences to lead, mentor, and support those affected by relationships that have not been healthy for them. Narcissistic abuse, emotional abuse, and psychological abuse are often brushed over because many do not understand the extensive emotional damage that is perpetuated within that abusive cycle. I know, I understand, I have been there.

My upbringing seemed perfect, calm, loving, and happy. How could I go from one extreme to another so quickly? I have asked myself that question a thousand times, and each time I have been unable to answer it. More than twenty-five years of my past have involved relationships that were not healthy for me. Lies, blame, isolation, criticism, control, and fear ruled my every move for over half my life. Those closest to me were deeply affected by this toxicity as well, while I watched from my paralyzed state, too afraid to choose myself and change my life.

Being in a toxic environment for this lengthy amount of time not only altered my values, but also caused me to adapt to my environment. The mistreatment became normal to me because I was exposed to it so often. The abuse, control, and danger seemed less intense because I became familiar with it. People outside did not understand, and my support system became very small as I tried to please, do better, and seek approval from the toxic people in my life. I found myself on a treadmill, trying to accommodate, change, help, be good enough and smart enough... only to find myself in the exact same place that I started in. Sometimes even worse.

Criticism and mistrust took a toll on my self-worth, leading me to believe that I would always fall short of someone's expectations and that maybe this was all I deserved. Years passed and I became used to the secluded lifestyle. Until one day, when someone came into my life offering me a chance at freedom. His past was similar in ways to mine and he could relate with my experiences. Because of that support, I began to seek awareness and education; beginning to understand the situations I had been in. Through that knowledge I gained empowerment. Slowly, learning what I deserved and why I had been robbed of it made the complete difference in my life.

This life was not exactly what I expected, but it is exactly what I needed to go through to be an inspiration of hope to those walking a path similar to my own. It is now my mission to help as many people as I can become aware of the character traits of the toxic person and emotional abuser. Extensive understanding of their characteristics and why they do the things they do leads to empowerment and ultimately, freedom.

Self-discovery and the rebuilding of one's self-worth after the toxic teardown is an essential part of healing and invaluable to those stepping out of a situation where they were controlled by another. My past is an example of a life that was a repetitive cycle of emotional and narcissistic abuse. Without someone to teach and support my healing, I would hate to see where I and those I love would be today.

I understand now that everything happens just the way it is supposed to. Because of my past, I have developed the ability to understand the toxic person extensively, to predict their behavior, to lead, guide, and encourage those still finding their path of purpose. I believe with all my heart that my life was lived in preparation to help those suffering today. Because toxic people do not change, it is our responsibility to change the way we allow toxic people to affect us.

Narcissistic and emotional abuse can be devastating. It is my hope that you will pass my information along to anyone that you feel may be in a relationship of any type that may not be healthy for them. Everyone needs someone to understand. My life has allowed me to understand many stories and facilitate change for others so that they can live the life they were meant to live.

It is said, "Nothing leaves our lives until we have learned what it has come to teach us." I will never stop learning, and from the way my life looks now, I don't have a choice. The person that entered my life at the exact time I needed the strength to find my freedom now shares my life in marriage. My husband gave me the greatest gift I could imagine. Although I did ALL the heavy lifting, he was present to support me. Because of this gift, I intend to pay it forward to my clients and those in my life who are searching find their freedom! You can always lift a bigger load when you are supported. YOU ARE NOT ALONE! You can feel the freedom.

Feel the Freedom

Dr. Heidi Brocke is a twenty-two-year doctor of chiropractic, acupuncturist, and advanced nutritionist who is branching out into the toxic relationship healing space. Her personal experiences compelled her to begin helping those whose lives have been affected by toxic relationships, narcissistic abuse, and emotional abuse.

Dr. Heidi presents at workshops and conferences, educating people about the nature of unhealthy relationships and how to reclaim their lives. She provides individual coaching and shares her programs with wider audiences online. Her latest, *"Freedom…Me!!!,"* is a comprehensive online program, available soon for purchase at coachingwithdrheidi.com.

Dr. Heidi has been interviewed as an expert on toxic relationship healing on television and radio, and is a regular contributor to magazine and newspaper articles and books on the subject.. In June 2018, *Time* magazine recognized Dr. Heidi for her groundbreaking work and tireless dedication to her clients.

Dr. Heidi owns a wellness center in the St. Louis area. She coaches clients near and far at her center, over the phone, and on video calls. Her mission is to bring hope, healing, and freedom to those whose lives have been affected by toxic relationships.

Continued…

Dr. Heidi Brocke
www.coachingwithdrheidi.com
drheidi@coachingwithdrheidi.com
www.facebook.com/coachingwithdrheidi
www.Instagram.com/coachingwithdrheid
Podcast "It's Not Normal. It's Toxic" is available on iTunes and Apple Podcast

DENA B. TRANEN

Minding Your Way

"We are not going to get in his way. If he makes it, we will take care of him and if he doesn't, we will grieve him." This was the decision we made after a sleepless night at the Ritz Carlton in St. Louis. Daniel went for a run in Forrest Park, he came back with a calm almost resolved look on his face and he asked me, "Isn't parenting a lot about learning to let go of control?". From there, we began our discussion about what do with our high risk, low odds, nineteen-week pregnancy.

Two days before this conversation we got the opinion of a senior OB in the hospital where I was being taken care of. While he was most well-known for his poor bedside manner, he was also a well-established expert in the field. His opinion was that since a catastrophic chain of events had already been set in motion, and since this child was relatively easy to conceive, we should end this pregnancy and start over. Basically, a cold "better luck next time," I guess.

My actual OB was a young compassionate doctor and a mom herself. She spoke powerful words of hope and humility to me in a calm and unexcited voice. Yet, even she agreed that the odds were not in our favor. It was suggested to us that we had a 10-20% chance the pregnancy would survive to viability. Normally I would not pursue something that had an 80-90% chance of failure, but I also knew the is decision looming before me was not that simple.

This all began when I woke up bleeding in the middle of the night at thirteen weeks. There was no clear answer from the ER as to what happened. There was still a heartbeat. They told me to go home and not lift anything heavy. The next five weeks were kind of a blur. I tried to honor my instincts that there really was a real problem with my pregnancy while accepting the reality that there was nothing I could do and nothing more would be known until the eighteen week anatomical evaluation.

My sister was with me for the eighteen week ultrasound. Our playful and light-hearted banter quickly shifted as the technician struggled to get any meaningful measurements. The technician left the room without saying much and a senior OB came in with a somber tone and a devastating printout for me to bring across the hall to review with my doctor. Inter-uterine growth restriction (IUGR), low amniotic fluid and evidence of placental abruptions. As I read that I went numb until I heard my doctor tell me I had time to think about things and make a decision. I knew I was crying and I remember thinking, "what does she mean, make a decision?".

I started to think about all of the decisions I had made in my life up to that point and how each decision led me down a certain path to this exact moment. The places I lived and traveled to, the people I loved and let go of until I loved Daniel and knew almost immediately that I would never let go of him. I thought about my choice to go to college at George Washington University in Washington, DC which led me to volunteer at the DC Rape Crisis Center which led me to know that connecting with people in their most vulnerable moments and being a part of their healing, was going to be my life's work. And now I had a new decision to make. I had to watch this seemingly hopeless pregnancy unfold week to week until ultimately I would have choose to either let it go or risk a world of terrifying unknowns.

I was frantic to find some answers about what we could be facing. What happens when a baby is born at twenty-six weeks? Twenty-eight weeks? One pound? Two pounds? What kinds of challenges does a child with a start like this have to deal with? Could I do it? Should I do it?

That next week was almost unbearable. We decided to keep a previously-scheduled trip to St. Louis to visit with Daniel's family. At dinner, my sister-in-law announced the reason she wasn't drinking was because she was pregnant. I knew she wanted to have more children and I had a moment of real joy for her. But then it hit me, waves and waves of grief that led to a night full of tears and rage until Daniel and I made our decision the next morning.

"We are not going to get in his way." This became a sort of mantra for us, a reasonable plan conjured up by expecting parents trying to understand parenthood and the desire to do right by their child. What I didn't really come to understand until a few years later is that my mantra wasn't just "we are not going to get in his way." My mantra was "I am not going to get in my own way."

I am not going to get in my own way. I wanted this baby to make it. I wanted to meet him. I wanted to be his mom. I almost let fear and self-doubt get in my way. On some level I knew if my son did survive to viability he would have some kind of challenge or disability. I knew that no one could come into the world so early and so small and in such distress and be "fine." I had no idea what was to come, but I was not going to get in my way of finding out.

At this point in my life I had been a therapist for over ten years. I taught mindfulness along with other skills to people with severe trauma, suicidality, eating disorders and personality disorders. I understood mindfulness. It made sense to me intellectually. I knew it was evidenced-based. I knew how it worked.

It wasn't until after we returned from our visit to St. Louis that I really got it. I remember the moment I felt it in my bones, mindfulness was how I was going to survive. I had no answers, I had no control, I had only my breath. Every day I had moments of fear and rage. What was going to happen? Why was it happening to me? As I noticed these thoughts I would place my hand on my still pregnant belly, I felt it expand as I inhaled and contract as I exhaled. I told myself "in this moment I am okay," "in this moment breathing is enough." I learned to lean in to the discomfort, distress and not knowing. I learned that there was nothing that I couldn't breath through. I learned to be a better and more present therapist.

In 2015, when my son was six months old, we moved to St. Louis. In 2016, I opened a private therapy and consulting practice. People often come into my office during the darkest moments in their lives. They come in at end of a marriage that stole their voice, the week after wrapping their car around a tree, the months after their child is diagnosed with a disability or disease. These are the moments we breath through.

The way out of the darkness and forward towards a better life starts with breathing through the pain, surviving what feels unbearable. The more we do this, the more we start to believe we can. Slowly over time, a deep reservoir of hope and trust builds from within.

Breathing is just the start. Next, begins the work of getting out of your own way. Quieting and challenging the voices in your head that say you can't, you shouldn't. You start to look at what you have been through and how you survived. You run through the choices you have made and how those decisions have led you to this exact moment. You breathe. You make the decision that fear and self-doubt will not rule your life and no matter what, you really will be okay; because, you actually are already okay.

And then, finally, you can breathe in the reality that freedom and possibility have no bounds and your capacity for love and healing is endless.

Dena B. Tranen, MSW, LCSW. Dena is a graduate of The George Warren Brown School of Social Work at Washington University in St. Louis. She began her career working with survivors of rape and sexual assault and homeless women in Washington, DC. She went on to work as a clinical social worker at the Harvard-affiliated McLean Hospital in Belmont, MA. While at McLean she received advanced training in DBT (Dialectal Behavior Therapy), MBT (Mentalization-Based Treatment) and CBT (Cognitive Behavioral Therapy). She has extensive experience working with adults and teenagers dealing with mood and trauma-related disorders, grief and life transitions.

While at McLean Dena developed expertise in the area of diagnosing and treating personality disorders, particularly borderline personality disorder and narcissistic personality disorder. She offers consultations with persons who have a personality disorder, with family members who have loved ones with a personality disorder, and with attorneys who have cases that involve person(s) with a personality disorder. Dena also works with people who have experienced trauma (PTSD), anxiety, depression and eating disorders. She presents regularly to audiences and at conferences throughout the country on these subjects and has appeared as an expert guest on St. Louis Public Radio.

Continued...

Dena currently owns and serves as Clinical Director for Middle Way Counseling and Consulting in St. Louis, MO. In addition to continuing to work as a therapist, she is trained as a coach in the collaborative divorce process and is an active member of the St. Louis Collaborative Family Law Association. She is currently conducting research in the area of marital resiliency in couples with a special needs or disabled child. She is known for her direct and interactive approach to therapy and is grateful to be a part of so many people's healing journeys.

Dena B Tranen, LCSW
www.middlewaystl.com

The Middle Way Counseling and Consulting
7751 Carondelet Ave, Suite 203
Clayton, MO 63105

ANNA-MARIE BEARD

And That's Okay

One morning, after dropping my son Tobin off at school, another mom and I pulled our cars together so we could talk and catch up. I remember the conversation so clearly.

Tobin had been attending a special school for children on the autism spectrum. He had been attending his school for almost a year; and on this particular morning, this sweet mom and I were talking through our car windows, catching up for a few moments.

She was talking about potty-training with her son. (Her son and Tobin were in the same class at the time.) She was sharing all of these really great strategies for potty training and how they were working with her son. And I was feeling myself filling up with excitement over the possibilities. Then when I was fully inflated with hope, suddenly reality sank in and I felt myself deflating inside, while still maintaining a smile, hoping my insides couldn't be seen from the outside:

There is **no way** Tobin is ready for any of this. He's four years old. And I don't know if he even understands when he is going to the bathroom. Familiar desperation started to fill me up—my heart pounding and I pictured myself changing his diaper when he is fourteen. And twenty-four. And thirty-four. Palms sweating and my insides start to sink into the big hole of the unknowns and what-ifs of the future.

Suddenly, I'm brave and I say in a very small voice, "I don't think Tobin understands when he is going to the bathroom. I don't even think he

has any realization." And she looks at me. Right in the eyes, smiling the same smile she had before, never missing a beat:
"And that's okay."

I can't adequately express what those words meant to me. It was acknowledgment. Permission to *feel*. Safety. Hope.
"It's *okay*."
I've read that sometimes parents of children with autism can be challenging to talk with because it seems like no one can say the right thing. We get upset easily or we get defensive. If we express something challenging and people respond with something trite, we can feel as though we have been dismissed. But if people respond by acting as though our child is shocking or disturbing or appalling, we have our claws out.

And I think this is very true. At least for me.

I can remember when I first knew Tobin's behaviors were atypical. I would express our challenges to people and some would respond with their own version. For example, I would share examples of Tobin's severe meltdowns. Someone would respond with *their* story of *their* child's meltdowns.

And I would **know** the person was trying to relate and calm my fears. But inside I would still feel a desperate, panicky feeling creep up:

They think I'm crazy.

I must be crazy.

No, I'm not crazy. I just can't handle this.

That's what it is. I'm not good enough or strong enough to handle this. Because this is hard for me.

Yep. That's it. I'm not enough.

No. No, it's that I'm crazy.

But then? At the same time, if someone responded to my story with that *look*? The one where I can tell the person is shocked or disgusted or *too* sympathetic or if they respond with a question like, "Did you know his diagnosis… *before* the adoption…?" My blood would boil and I would rage inside as the mama bear fought to claw herself out.

It was like no one could really say the right thing.

I've been thinking on this lately.

Because I think maybe this is true for anyone going through something hard, processing something hard, and transitioning to a new normal. Those moments when the ground has shaken and everything is topsy-turvy, and you're finding a new way to navigate through the world.

It's like no one can say the right thing.

And I think that's okay.

Too often we get so bogged down with fear of not *saying* the right thing or *doing* the right thing—so we don't do *anything*.

Some friends and I were talking about this recently. My friend Nikki brought up a Jewish custom called "sitting Shiva." This is the period of seven days following the death of a loved one where the bereaved sit for seven days, while friends and family visit to offer condolences, share stories of the deceased, and be together. The idea is to come alongside the grieving, to "empower the community to be God's partner in comforting those who mourn." Sometimes they don't say anything at all. Sometimes they just sit with the bereaved. But they sit—***together***.

This custom is specifically for someone grieving the death of a loved one, but the message behind it grips me because of what it communicates:

You are not alone. I am *with* you.

Sometimes when you are going through something hard, that's all you need to hear. Or *feel*.

Maybe sometimes we put too much pressure on ourselves or on others to "say the right thing."

Because when someone you love is going through something hard and you know it's hard and the hard is making **them** hard to be around… What *do you* say? What *can* you say? What's the *right thing* to say? That's a lot of pressure. On ourselves and on others.

And pressure like that can actually lead to inactivity.

Maybe it's not so much about what you communicate verbally but what you communicate through action.

I'm a Harry Potter fan, and I can't help but think of the moment in the movie *Order of the Phoenix* when Luna comforts Harry by squeezing his hand. They are standing in the corridor; she offers condolences and reaches out and squeezes his hand for a moment… then lets it go. It's Luna's way of communicating, "I'm here. I'm with you."

I think when we're going through hard things, we can be incredibly difficult to talk with, even if we're good at hiding our twisted up insides with a smile on our face.

Words *can* sting. But no acknowledgment can, too.

Because hard is not necessarily *bad*. It's just hard.

And Good *can* come from hard. But the hard is still hard.

My son Tobin is a light to my life and my family's life. And to all who really know him. He brings joy and laughter and understanding of the big important secrets of life that would have remained hidden to me if it weren't for Tobin.

But some things about the way autism affects Tobin are challenging.

And that's okay.

The hard my husband and I have been through? I *never* want to go through that again.

And that's okay.

But the *after*? The new life we are filled with? The fresh breath that keeps moving through our family? I wouldn't trade that for anything. It's game-changing Good. And just keeps getting better every single day.

And that's okay.

And That's Okay

When we are in the midst of hard, we may have the "head knowledge" that Good can come out of it, but we may not have the "heart knowledge." We may know but not **know**.

I'm an optimist. It's engrained in me to see the bright side of things. So I'm fully aware that I can be incredibly annoying to someone who needs to just sit in the dark.

I want to get better at this.

And I want to get better at being still.

At finding my own unique way to sit Shiva with someone hurting.

I want to be okay with not knowing what to say but still moving, still taking a step toward someone's hurt.

I think sometimes we just need to know *we're* okay. And even if what we're going through is *not* okay, that's okay, too.

I think sometimes it might just be about saying to someone, "I know you're going through something hard. And you don't have to say or do anything. Just know I am here. I am *with* you." Sometimes this is with words. Sometimes it's a squeeze of the hand.

But sometimes… oftentimes, it's simply saying:

"And that's okay."

Anna-Marie Beard is an ordinary mom of two extraordinary boys, one of whom is on the autism spectrum. Life took an adventurous turn when she and her husband Brian adopted their two little boys from Korea.

She spends her time in transportation (as she drives her son to a school for autism two hours away), yoga, writing, and taking care of her family. She regards her three boys as her greatest gifts, and writes about the Good that comes during both the hards and highs of life on their family blog: www.pursuingtob.com.

With a bachelor's degree in secondary education English and a master's in English, she taught high school and college writing. She also worked as a creative director for her church. She has been featured on the Prentke Romich Company blog (https://www.prentrom.com/articles/tob-worlds-creating-words?mode=view&header=caregivers) and is a frequent contributor to the AAC Language Lab blog: https://aaclanguagelab.com/blog/better where she shares the real-life experiences of their non-verbal son's progress on his communication device.

A recovering perfectionist, Anna-Marie devotes her time and her writing to pursuing "tob," the Hebrew word meaning "good" or "goodness." The imperfect. The dynamic. The messy. She examines her life to find the wonder, growth, and love that come from some of the messiest, vulnerable moments, and then shares those moments with the world because she believes the sacred spaces are in the midst of hard. In the simple moments of the everyday. The mountains and the valleys. Her work is an attempt to live a life in constant pursuit of the Good.

Anna-Marie Beard
www.pursuingtob.com
a-m.beard@outlook.com
www.instagram.com/anna-marieandbrian
www.youtube.com/channel/UCa84Jf-c7ENdrVuJ5h8Rw6g

CYNTHIA STEINERT

The Leap

Have you ever felt like you're in the wrong the place? You know there's something more you should be doing but you can't figure out what that is. I felt that way for many years. I was a single mom of one and I had a secure job working for the government. They pay was good, the benefits were ok and the best part was that I'd been there so long I knew how to do my job like the back of my hand. As much I don't like to admit it, I also knew how to manipulate the system. But…. I hated it, I hated every minute of it.

I was brought up with the mindset that working 9-5 was the only way to make a living but I've always had visions of being a business owner. Over the years, business ideas came and went but I muddled along in my mundane well paying job, that I hated, because I had no idea how to take the leap.

Then it happened…. A favorite place of mine called Silver Lining was preparing to close. One of my mentors said to me, Silver Lining is closing at the end of the year. My response was "No It's Not". Not realizing what I had said, I went on about my life for the next couple weeks and eventually the lightbulb went off. Oh my God, Everything in my world was pointing toward Silver Lining but I couldn't see how to make it work. So, I drug my feet.

Have you ever been given an opportunity or idea and thrown one road block after another in the way? Well, that was me too but the universe would have no part of that. With little to no money in the bank, no retail experience and zero business experience I was pushed forward. Trust me, I went along on this ride kicking and screaming. Every road block was mysteriously removed and I intuitively knew that this was my path. The day I closed on the purchase December 22, 2017, I grabbed a bottle of wine, sat in the middle of the floor at Silver Lining and cried because I was already exhausted and had no idea how this was going to work. I still had my full time job and now I had to figure out how to run a business.

Still unsure of how this was going to work, I opened the doors on January 2, 2018. I had lined up someone to work the front desk while I continued to work my mundane job. One week into it, I thought I was going to die. I was exhausted. Two weeks into it, I was notified that the government contract I had been working under for 20+ years was coming to an end on January 18, 2018. A blessing in disguise or curse? I knew I couldn't do both for long but I lived in a beautiful loft in downtown St. Louis which I refer to as the high rent district and I had no idea how I was going to pay the bills without that full time job. Granted I was offered another position within the organization that I was working for but I would've had to take a huge pay cut. So, I said to myself, if you're going to take a pay cut then take the entire pay cut. In all honesty, I couldn't have done both at the same time and been successful at either one for very long.

On January 18, 2018, I said my goodbyes to the fulltime job and went all in at Silver Lining. There I was in a world I knew very little about and a community I knew nothing about trying to figure out the ins and outs of running a small business. The days were long and exhausting but there were people everywhere trying to support my efforts and help in any way they could. It didn't take long for me to realize that I needed to make this journey on my own. Too many hands in the pot was creating problems with inventory and the cash drawer amongst several other things. I needed to learn all the processes myself so that I could teach others how things should flow and set some boundaries for those who wanted to help. That being said, my days got longer and my stress level went through the roof. There were a couple of days that I sat in the middle of Silver Lining and screamed "If this is how it's going to be then I'm out". I'm not sure who I was talking to besides the universe, but knowing that this was my path I intuitively knew that everything was going to be ok. So, I continued to show up every day and give a 100%. My heart was all in but my body was struggling. There's definitely something about doing what you love that keeps you going.

In the first six months of owning Silver Lining, I dealt with broken Processes and systems, legal discrepancies, serious plumbing issues and personality conflicts to name a few. I gained a ton of new friends and some enemies too. I made thousands of mistakes and learned hundreds of things the hard way. I had so many balls in the air every day that I felt like a failure most days but I was happier than I'd ever been and somehow, at the end of the day, everything seemed to work itself out. The universe had my back. So, I pushed forward.

Adding insult to injury, On June 30th, the lease on my loft was coming up for renewal and they wanted to hike up the rent. So there I was, already feeling like the rent was too high and not having any steady income I decided it was time to move. Moving in itself is stressful much less for someone who is a new business owner. Not only did I not have time to look for a place I also had no proof of income. At one point, I thought I had rendered myself homeless because I had already declined renewing my lease and there didn't seem to be a solution to my living arrangements. At the very least, I knew I could sleep at Silver Lining but that wasn't exactly where I saw myself at 49 years old. Several people offered me a space in their home but that wasn't feeling right either. I had my ego in the way. Two days before my move out date, the universe stepped in again and I graciously accepted an offer from one of my mentors to move into the lower level of her home. It was a huge blessing. Once the move was complete my stress level started to decline and life became simpler.

Things started to level off at Silver Lining as I learned the systems, put boundaries in place and had a bed to sleep in which gave me time to breath and allowed me to get some much needed selfcare. In addition, I finally had time to ponder the vision of what Silver Lining was to become. While my stress level went down the amount of work that needed to be done did not. I worked seven days a week ten hours a day to keep up with all the demands but I loved it.

Through that experience, I grew immensely. It was painful most days and the lessons were grueling but oh so rewarding at the end of each day. So, here I sit with no financial security to speak of, living in the lower level of a home that belongs to one of my mentors and I've never been happier. I work a lot of hours and try to keep a lot people happy because I believe in what Silver Lining brings to the table and I don't regret a thing.

At the end of the day, Our paths are already laid out for us. Ideas are given to us by the Universe for a reason. If we don't listen and go gracefully we will eventually be pushed hard enough by the Universe to get on the path. So, take the leap. It's well worth it. I have no idea where this journey will take me but I'm definitely all in and know for sure that the Universe has my back.

The Leap

Cynthia Steinert is the owner of Silver Lining—A Healing Home, A Holistic Wellness Center, and Boutique.

As the owner of Silver Lining she encourages all forms of Holistic Health and Wellness. Her goal is to facilitate healing and educate the masses on healthy eating, the use of essential oils, the power of our energetic fields, empathic behaviors and the value of meditation and yoga amongst many other things. Her vision for Silver Lining is one of healing and community.

She graduated with a bachelors degree in Information Systems and spent 20 plus years working as a Network Engineer for the Department of Defense before taking on the ownership of Silver Lining. She is now dedicated to changing people's lives via The Healing Home known as Silver Lining.

Cynthia Steinert
314-548-2999
cynthia@silverliningstl.com
www.silverliningstl.com

www.facebook.com/cindy.steinert
www.facebook.com/silverliningstl/
www.instagram.com/cindy.steinert
www.instagram.com/silverliningstl

REBECCA NOW

American Women Speak Up

Through three centuries, American women have struggled to have their voices heard.

In 1968, when I was a teenager, I first read Betty Freidan's *The Feminine Mystique* written in 1963. I cried, seeing my mother's story in its pages. I read the book again several years ago and cried once more recognizing my mother's struggles long after she had passed on. *The Feminine Mystique* woke women up in America to see their personal angst and frustrations as cultural forces that could be changed. My mother struggled with depression, isolation and a dislike of her role as housewife and mother. When I would come home from school as a child I never knew who I would meet when I opened the front door. Would she be playing opera music and be happy? Would she be weeping in the back room? Would she be sullen and angry? She later went to treatment for depression and was given electric shock treatment. I couldn't get out of the house soon enough when I left home for college. I threw myself into friendships and studies and was determined to build a life for myself that was "not my mother."

After college, I left my hometown of St. Louis, Missouri, for California and spent 27 years there. I was determined to have a successful career and not end up trapped in the dreaded housewife role. I was largely successful delaying motherhood until I was 41 years old, having only one child.

I remember coming home to St. Louis when my dad was ill in 2001. He had suffered from Alzheimer's for some time and was doing poorly. When I walked off the elevator at the rehabilitation center, I saw a man slumped in a wheelchair. I said to myself, "Oh that poor man!" I started to walk past him, and an instant flash of recognition came across me, "Oh my God, that's my dad!" My dad had become a shadow of his former self. His lungs and heart were functioning, but his mind was gone. He was utterly unable to communicate. It was a shocking site for me. I was at the rehab center with my mom. My dad wasn't communicating and I'm trying to get a grip on my raging sorrow, wanting to cry out "Who took my dad? Where is my dad? He's not here." I calmed myself, and then I looked over at my mother. I realized I could never ask my father questions about his youth, his upbringing, things that were important to him. I would never be able to talk to him again because he was beyond communication. But my mother was there. She was fully functioning, and I decided to seize the moment. "Mom," I said, "What was the highlight of your life?"

She paused and then told me the highlight of her life was being on the high school debate team and having the lead in a high school play. She got very happy discussing these memories. I was shocked. She was 80 years old and the highlight happened when she was a teenager? I thought for sure the happiest memories had something to do with the four daughters she raised. Wasn't that the highlight of her life? I realized that inside her was someone who wanted to express herself. Like many women in the post-World War II era, she fell into the culture of motherhood and domestic goddess that was part of 1950s suburban America. An experience that was so eloquently brought to life by Betty Freidan's book.

A part of me has always wanted to heal my mother, in some child-like way. I sometimes think I became more self-expressed, by speaking, and writing, because my Mother seemed to have been excluded from those endeavors.

American Women Speak Up

If women's lack of opportunities in the mid-20th century of my mother's time were stifling, peeking into the early 19th century when two women dared to speak in public is even more enlightening. Sarah Grimke grew up in antebellum Charleston, South Carolina in a wealthy household with slaves. Sarah was depressed and went through a time of inner turmoil before deciding to become a Quaker, leaving her family to journey North and advocate for abolishing slavery.

Later bringing her sister Angelina to join her, the two sisters became public speakers against the institution of slavery, hired as agents by the American Anti-Slavery Society. Because they had the personal experience of living in a household with slaves, their voices resonated with Northerners. However, women in 1837 were not supposed to speak in public but defer to their husbands. It was declared by scripture and every preacher would rail against women speaking in front of a 'mixed' audience (men and women together). When the two women were hired as speaking agents for the anti-slavery movement, they spoke to women in parlors. However, they became so popular that bigger and bigger halls had to be secured for people to hear them speak. Their audience consisted of women and men as well. The two women received an amazing amount of vicious bullying through the media of the era—the newspapers.

Flash forward to the 21st century. My own journey toward self-expression was a step by step progression, stumbling along the way. After determining to be "not as miserable as my mother," I became quite career focused. Two things that have helped me: self-development classes and great role models. Looking back, I was sensitive to criticism during my college years, and would withdraw at any push back. I once gave a talk as a sophomore at Mizzou on women's bodies as advertising tools, and someone wrote a letter to the campus paper criticizing my ideas. It totally shut me down. I withdrew from the conversation and activities. After my first marriage ended in divorce when I was 28, I took a class at the San

Francisco Learning Annex on assertiveness training, and today still use the techniques I learned. My career at Macy's department stores, steadily climbed, and I enjoyed great mentors and colleagues that were powerful, self-expressed women. I discovered new ways of thinking about the human experience, through Landmark Education and New Thought. Step by step, I grew in awareness and confidence.

The powerful catapult forward was propelled through Toastmaster's International. The organization is world-wide, and helps develop confidence, communication skills and leadership. Starting as a somewhat hesitant, unorganized speaker, with a propensity to use filler words, such as 'um' and 'ah', I slowly grew in confidence and skill over 5 years. Speaking weekly in front of an encouraging group was the key. I started competing in speaking contests and had a bit of success, taking first place in a division contest in 2014. The ultimate prize for any competitive speaker was to go to the Toastmaster's International Convention and compete for World Champion of Public Speaking. The contest has been around since 1938. In 90 years, only 5 women have won the coveted top prize. Of course, part of the abysmal record is made worse by the knowledge that before 1973, women were not even allowed to be part of Toastmasters. It was a male only organization.

One year, I fell out of competition for the speech contest, and I volunteered as a judge at a division contest. A woman gave the most eloquent, beautiful personal story of her escape from an abusive relationship. It touched and moved me, I thought she was easily the best speaker, and my ballot reflected her status as the best. I was astonished when the results of the judge's ballots (there were 5 of us) were counted, and she did not win. I started to notice the gender of the judges and wondered if women's stories did not resonate with male judges. I watched the finalists in the World Championship of Public Speaking contest via live streaming for several years, and the winners, consistently for years, all seemed to be men. Occasionally a stray woman would make it to second place.

When I went to the World Championship of Public Speaking contest in August, 2018 all of that changed. Ten contestant finalists spoke on the stage in Chicago, Illinois, six men and four women. History was made when Ramona J. Smith took first place, Sherrie Su took second place, and Anita Fain Taylor placed third. Three women won the top three spots. A triple header and I was there to witness history. Champion Ramona J. Smith used boxing as her metaphor for life, and opened her speech with these words:

"Life will sometimes feel like a fight. The punches, jabs and hooks will come in the form of challenges, obstacles and failure, yet if you stay in the ring and learn from those past fights, at the end of each round, you will be still standing."

These last three centuries of women finding their voices have been fraught with challenges, obstacles, and failure. Yet for American women from Sarah Grimke in 1837 to my mother in the 1960's, to my journey into confidence and self-expression, and the World Champion Ramona J. Smith in 2018, we not only are still standing, but still speaking and encouraging others to do the same.

Hear Her Now

It is rare for one individual to have lived and breathed in three centuries. **Rebecca Now** is an award-winning international speaker, and a guest columnist for the St. Louis Women's Journal. She speaks on women's empowerment and self-expression, as well as the history of the U.S. Women's Movement. She is also a historical re-enactor for Elizabeth Cady Stanton.

She came of age during the 'second wave' of feminism in the 1970's, is a recommitted activist in the 21st century 'third wave', and, performs as a re-enactor for a 19th century trail blazer. She claims affinity to all three waves of feminism.

Rebecca Now
314 800-4050
rebeccanow@sbcglobal.net
www.rebeccanowandthen.com